The Patriot's Progress

wet winter conditions in and around Ploegsteert Wood and was invalided home in January 1915. When commissioned into the Machine Gun Corps in April, Williamson's formal connection with the LRB was at an end. However, he did attend several reunion luncheons, claiming erroneously on at least two occasions that he had been the battalion's youngest member to sail on the *Chyebassa*. It is very likely that during these gatherings he learned the fate of many of his Sun Fire Insurance colleagues with whom he had served in P Company. Most of those former comrades who were not killed or wounded when the battalion was more than decimated during Second Ypres became casualties at Gommecourt on 1 July 1916. Actions near Kansas Cross and Wieltje cost the LRB over 130 fatalities and the diversionary attack against the Gommecourt salient, 286 dead.

Williamson is known to have read many of the books written after the war by fellow survivors. It is possible that he came across *The Somme* and *The Coward* written by Donald Gristwood, another former member of the LRB, erstwhile insurance clerk and resident of a south-east London suburb. Gristwood and Williamson built the stories of their central characters around their own personal experiences. Both authors had fought on the Somme, had been wounded and had suffered severe difficulties readjusting to civilian life.

John Bullock's initial commitment to the war was reflected across the class divides of Edwardian Britain. The often prolonged wait for overseas active service did little to dilute the enthusiasm of the volunteers. If anything, and despite the growing casualty lists and the increasing domestic demands of total war, it served to sharpen their desire to get to the front and fulfil their duty or dreams. The disastrous Gallipoli campaign, the disappointment of Loos, alarm at the East coast bombardments, the disruption caused by Zeppelin raids, the introduction of conscription and the mobilisation of Britain's industrial capacity had convinced many before 1916 that the war was not to be over quickly. Nevertheless, there was a widespread belief among the volunteers and conscripts of 1916 that a victory for the citizen armies then flooding into France was inevitable. Although they might not have offered their services earlier, conscripts were not necessarily unpatriotic or apathetic. Many men preferred to wait and earn better money in

INTRODUCTION

K.W. Mitchinson

When war broke out in August 1914, several hundred thousand young and not so young men flocked to enlist in the Territorials and Kitchener's New Armies. The patriotic fervour and clamour to take the King's shilling continued well into 1915 and by the end of the year nearly two and a half million men had volunteered to serve. Impressive and unimagined as this figure was, it had become apparent that the nation could no longer rely purely upon the voluntary movement. As Britain continued to develop its capacity to wage total war, new means and methods had to be introduced to ensure that the unprecedented size of the BEF could be sustained in the field by a regular and consistent flow of new recruits.

Henry Williamson's John Bullock was one of Kitchener's first 100,000. Instead of the anticipated hasty posting to France followed by a rapid march on Berlin, much of the new army spent many frustrating months training on such places as Salisbury Plain or Cannock Chase. When he was eventually drafted in the early autumn of 1916, 'Everysoldier' joined a battalion serving on the Western Front. Bullock, like so many of the 1914 and 1915 enlistments, travelled to France with feelings of relief, anticipation and dread. Soon after joining his battalion it moved south to the Somme. Here Bullock experienced the mud, slime and blasted woods of the chalklands before next seeing service in the equally demoralising and soul-destroying slough of the Salient. By the time he lost a leg in 1917, Bullock's battalion had undergone transitions common to most units of the BEF. It was no longer a battalion of volunteers, but one comprised largely of Derby men and conscripts.

Williamson's own period of training in the Weald and of his service in France provided much of the raw material for John Bullock's subsequent 'progress'. In January 1914 Williamson had enlisted in the London Rifle Brigade, an exclusive Territorial regiment, and had embarked with the battalion for France on 4 November of the same year. He suffered from the bitterly cold and

First published in 1930 by Geoffrey Bles

First published in this edition in 1999 by
Sutton Publishing Limited
Phoenix Mill · Thrupp · Stroud · Gloucestershire GL5 2BU
in association with the Imperial War Museum

British Library Cataloguing in Publication Data

ISBN 0 7509 2234 6

This is the eleventh in the *Arts and Literature* Series of facsimile
reprints produced by the Department of Printed Books, Imperial
War Museum

ALAN SUTTON™ and SUTTON™ are
thetrade marks of Sutton Publishing Limited

Printed in Great Britain by
The Guernsey Press Company Limited,
Guernsey, Channel Islands.

The Patriot's Progress

Being the Vicissitudes of Pte. John Bullock

HENRY WILLIAMSON

Drawings by William Kermode

SUTTON PUBLISHING
in association with the
IMPERIAL WAR MUSEUM

safer employment until they were called; when their name came up, they were as prepared to leave their families and homes as those who had gone before. There remained a strong sense of commitment to country and community, a desire to do what was expected of a Briton. For many soldiers and civilians, therefore, 1 July 1916 came as a profound shock.

A plethora of books later confirmed that the opening day of the Somme both marked a watershed in the nation's attitude towards the war and scored an indelible scar through its collective psyche. The volumes of poetry and 'anti-war' novels which appeared both during and after the war (many of which it should be remembered were published for commercial gain at a time when the nation's mood was susceptible to such sentiment), fuelled post-war generations' assumptions that almost every soldier who survived the Somme became disillusioned and demoralised. The evidence to confirm this belief was apparent in every line: the war was run by incompetent generals, indolent staff officers and grasping profiteers. The futility of the war itself and the stupidity with which it was waged also became the central tenets of numerous studies produced during the 1970s and early 1980s.

When John Bullock arrived at his battalion in September 1916 he joined a unit which had fought on 1 July. The survivors, according to Bullock, 'did not speak of it, except indirectly, by reference'. When drafts arrived to replace losses, adjutants of some battalions gave many surviving members jobs away from the front line companies. These originals became transport drivers, batmen, orderly room staff – a reward for having volunteered and survived. Nevertheless, there were still originals who remained in the front line. When away from the trenches, they often withdrew into small groups to share food parcels and seek comfort and comradeship from their collective experience. Newcomers posted to such sections or platoons initially felt isolated and ignored. They could expect to be given the dirtiest and most dangerous jobs and were often killed or maimed before anyone had asked or even discovered their names. As he was fortunate to remain with some friends of the same draft, John Bullock seems not to have suffered too much in this respect. However, the drudgery and cold of a Somme winter and the remorseless demands of trench warfare caused an increasing number of Bullock's comrades to become casualties. Like so many men in battalions, artillery brigades and field companies up and down the line, John Bullock was forced to confront the brutality of war with a diminishing number of those he knew and trusted.

Post-war research demonstrates that men quickly lost the ideals for which they might have originally enlisted. Nebulous notions of patriotic duty, King and country were replaced by a bond between men who suffered and endured together. Duty to country was overtaken by loyalty to their comrades and, to a lesser extent, their battalion. Despite the widespread belief that people at home did not, and could not, comprehend the travails through which the man at the front passed, and in spite of the number of times a battalion might be torn to shreds and rebuilt, the morale of the British soldier did not break. Although 1917 was a year of continued slaughter on land, sea and air, there remained a belief in ultimate victory. Lessons were being learned and technologies improved. Even the loss of the Russian 'steamroller', the introduction of rationing, the general war weariness and the shock of the German offensives in 1918, did not sap the will to resist. Many soldiers did feel betrayed, forgotten and neglected, did express with bitterness their resentment of the war and all that it involved, and dreamt of a return to quieter times. Nevertheless, millions of John Bullocks, albeit grousing as they went, fought on and won for themselves and for their comrades the remarkable victories of 1918.

K.W. Mitchinson, historian of the LRB Association, is the author of *Gentlemen and Officers: the impact and experience of war on territorial regiment 1914–1918*, published by the Imperial War Museum in 1995. This social history of a military unit was based on the Association's unique collection of albums, diaries, periodicals and photographs now residing in the Imperial War Museum, and constitutes a fascinating study of what it was really like to be in the army at that time. His other works include *Saddleworth 1914–1919: the experience of a Penine community during the Great War* (Saddleworth Historical Society, 1995); *Cotton town comrades: the story of the Oldham Pals Battalions, 1914–1919* with I. McInnes (Bayonet Publications, 1993) and *Pioneer Battalions in the Great War* (Leo Cooper, 1997).

BIOGRAPHICAL NOTE

Anne Williamson

The First World War was the pivot upon which the whole of Henry Williamson's life turned. It occupied his thoughts and dominated his actions throughout the rest of his eighty years and was the direct source for seven[1] of his fifty books as well as many articles on the subject, and the indirect source for much of his other writing.

The full story of his life can be found in my biography *Henry Williamson: Tarka and the Last Romantic*[2] but, although it is impossible to do justice to such a complicated man in such a small space, there follows a brief outline of his work to put this new edition of *The Patriot's Progress* into context.

Born on 1 December 1895 in south-east London, Henry was the middle child of William and Gertrude Williamson. His father was a bank clerk and the family and its lifestyle at that time was fairly mundane middle-class, into which the difficult boy fitted rather uneasily. Educated at Colfe's Grammar School, Henry left school in the summer of 1913 and commenced work as a clerk in the Sun Fire Insurance office, and one feels that his life could quite easily have been a repetition of that of his father. But the events of 1914 catapulted him, together with the whole country, into the eruption of the First World War.

Already enlisted into the London Rifle Brigade, Henry spent the first three months of the war training in earnest. His unit embarked for France on 5 November 1914. I have recorded the full story of his war service in my recent book *A Patriot's Progress: Henry Williamson and the First World War*.[3] Suffice it to state here that after being invalided home Williamson was commissioned into the Bedfordshire Regiment in April 1915, trained as a Transport Officer, returned to the front with 208 MGC in spring 1917, and later rejoined the Bedfordshires.

By the time of his demobilisation in September 1919 he had already determined to become a writer. Nearly 24 years old, with his recent experiences indelibly fixed in his mind, he realised the futility of war and determined that as a survivor his duty lay in being a voice for those who had died: to expose the causes of war and to find a way of ensuring that such a horrific situation could never occur again.

In March 1921, after eighteen months of friction in the family home, his first book was accepted for publication. After a final quarrel with his father, he rode on his Norton motorcycle down to Georgeham in north Devon where he had spent an idyllic holiday in May 1914 and established himself in the thatched cottage he named Skirr. He married in 1925 and spent his honeymoon visiting the battlefields. But it was not until after the publication in 1927 of *Tarka the Otter*[4] which brought him fame when it was awarded the Hawthornden Prize the following year, that he began to write directly about the war. The fact that 1928 was the tenth anniversary of the Armistice gave him the opportunity for an intense production of articles. He made another return visit to the battlefields in 1927, and articles arising from these visits were gathered into *The Wet Flanders Plain*, with its powerful opening 'Apologia pro mea Vita'.[5]

In 1928 Williamson was also asked to write some brief descriptive paragraphs to accompany lino-cuts of war scenes by the Tasmanian artist William Kermode, but he decided to write a full text, which resulted in *The Patriot's Progress*.[6] The combination of stark text and dramatic illustration provides an extraordinarily powerful exposition of the war machine – a record of a profound and terrible human experience. It is no coincidence that the title echoes John Bunyan's *A Pilgrim's Progress*, and direct analogy can be made between the two books. But Williamson's title is ironic: his hero does not 'progress'. The book's purpose is to show the total futility of war.

In the mid-1930s Henry Williamson felt he had written all he could about the West Country and, reading the portents of another war, he decided to buy a farm in Norfolk. Williamson's farming years during the Second World War were almost as traumatic as his experience of the trenches during the First World War.

The end of the war also brought the end of his marriage and Henry Williamson returned to Devon alone. But he soon met the lady who was to become his second wife. This gave him new impetus for writing and he embarked on the long-planned series of novels entitled *A Chronicle of Ancient Sunlight*.[7] Based to a very large extent on his own life and that of his parents, family and friends, the *Chronicle* encompasses a true historical (but fictionalised) record of life in Britain in the first half of the twentieth century, including five detailed volumes covering the First World War.

But his second marriage also ended in divorce and completion of his mammoth task exhausted him while the lack of recognition for his achievement depressed him. Despite the efforts of family and close friends he became a lonely old man. Taken into the care of the monks at Twyford Abbey on the outskirts of London, he died there on 13 August 1977. He is buried in Georgeham churchyard, in the shadow of the cottage that he had rented when he first went to live in Devon in 1921, and where he stayed in May 1914.

NOTES

1. The seven titles are: *The Wet Flanders Plain*, Faber, 1929; *The Patriot's Progress*, Geoffrey Bles, 1930; and the five 'war volumes' of *A Chronicle of Ancient Sunlight*: Vol. 4, *How Dear is Life*, Macdonald, 1954; Vol. 5, *A Fox under My Coat*, Macdonald, 1955; Vol. 6, *The Golden Virgin*, Macdonald, 1957; Vol. 7, *Love and the Loveless*, Macdonald, 1958; Vol. 8, *A Test to Destruction*, Macdonald, 1960. These five volumes are currently published in a paperback edition by Sutton Publishing.

2. Anne Williamson, *Henry Williamson: Tarka and the Last Romantic*, Sutton Publishing, 1995, pb edn 1997.

3. Anne Williamson, *A Patriot's Progress: Henry Williamson and the First World War*, Sutton Publishing, 1998. ISBN 0 7509 1339 8, £18.99.

4. Henry Williamson, *Tarka the Otter*, first published by Putnam, 1927. In print continously ever since.

5. Henry Williamson, *The Wet Flanders Plain*, Faber, 1929. 'Apologia pro mea Vita' originally appeared as a newspaper article 'I Believe in the Men who Died'. See Anne Williamson, *A Patriot's Progress*, op cit.

6. Henry Williamson, *The Patriot's Progress*, Geoffrey Bles, 1930; rev. edn. Macdonald, 1968. New edn Sutton Publishing, 1999.

7. Henry Williamson, *A Chronicle of Ancient Sunlight*, Macdonald Publishing, 1951–1969; reprinted 1984–5. All 15 volumes are currently available in paperback edition published by Sutton Publishing.

PAGE

FIRST PHASE - - - - - - - *One*

SECOND PHASE - - - - - - *Thirty-three*

THIRD PHASE - - - - - - *Eighty-five*

FOURTH PHASE - - *One-hundred-and-twenty-three*

FIFTH PHASE - - - *One-hundred-and-seventy-nine*

The idea of *The Patriot's Progress* grew from a suggestion, in 1928, that I should write captions for a set of lino-cuts which illustrated the Great War. The idea came from J. C. Squire, then editing *The London Mercury* from a small office in Fleet Street. " They are done by an Australian soldier who served, like yourself, on the Western Front," said Jack Squire " If you'd like to talk to him about it, we'll go into the pub next door."

The lino-cuts were almost caricatures, yet the details were real. I wanted the reality itself ; and after several meetings with the artist, William Kermode, a quickly perceptive chap, the proposal was made that, if he could see his way to scrapping some of the scenes and cutting new pictures, I'd write an entire story around them, pouring in a concrete of words making, as it were, a line of German mebus, or ' pillboxes ' of the kind which had frustrated our attacks during Third Ypres—that series of battles fought for the possession of the Passchendaele Ridge during the summer of 1917, which turned out to be the wettest in Flanders for forty years.

The German positions below the Ridge, which lay seven miles east of Ypres and was less than seventy metres above sea-level, had once been served by two single railway lines, upon which many thousands of tons of gravel from the Rhine had been brought to make low, massive concrete forts at strategic points. Farmhouse walls were used as shuttering to enclose concrete

three and four feet thick below roofs of ferro-
concrete of equal solidity, with low-placed
splayed slits for machine-gun cross-fire. Our
soldiers called them pill-boxes, after the small
round wooden boxes sold by chemists before the
war. They had names like Kronprinz, Vampir,
the Cockroft, and Tirpitz.

William Kermode, who had served in tanks
during Third Ypres, agreed enthusiastically with
this new idea. His lino-cuts would be shuttering
to my verbal concrete. Some of the original
pictures were replaced by new ones, to follow
the text. I was half-way through the slow,
laborious, and at times resented job of work
(resented for reasons to be recorded later) when
Mr. Constant Huntington, of Putnam & Co.,
sent me a bound page-proof of a book he was
shortly to publish. In a covering letter he
declared that it would sweep the world. It was
a translation of a German book to be called, in
English, *All Quiet on the Western Front*—a phrase
which often appeared in the communiqués from
G.H.Q. of the British Expeditionary Force.

I read about one third of the book, then put
it aside. One of the similes (I write from memory)
was ' like a fart on a curtain pole '. What this
meant I didn't bother to think : the book seemed
to me to be written with the imagined dread of
an inexperienced infantryman who had never
felt the release of tension during battle, when
action dissipates the terrors of pre-action. *All
Quiet* was not in the class of Barbusse's *Le Feu*,
Civilisation by Duhamel, Wilfrid Ewart's *Way
of Revelation*, or the poems of Sassoon, Blunden,
and Graves. If *All Quiet* was going to ' sweep
the world ', then—-

I abandoned P.P., one-third done. A year passed before it was taken up and finished ; meanwhile war-books of all kinds followed the phenomenal sales of *All Quiet*. The ' boom ' had ended with a hotchpotch entitled *Generals Die In Bed*, which out-farted the curtain pole to such an extent that *The Daily Mail* in a leading article called for its withdrawal.

When, at the end of 1929, I managed to complete the P.P. text, and showed it to the amiable and patient Bill Kermode, I said " By the way, have you ever been in the sort of brothel you have illustrated ? "

" No," he replied, adding that the only red lights he had seen ' over there ' were from S.O.S. rockets during a battle.

However, possibly there were such things, we agreed ; and so left in John Bullock's wretched yearning for the comfort of Mother Eve.

The Patriot's Progress was published in April 1930. War books were what was then called a drug on the market. To my surprise it was given prominence by Arnold Bennett in his famous *Books and Persons* page of *The Evening Standard* of May 8, 1930. And it had splendid reviews elsewhere. It was even serialised in *The Evening Standard*. The first edition was soon sold out. Two reprintings were called for during the following month.

I find a clipping of A.B.'s review in my 1930 copy.

There have been so many war books, and so many good war books, and so many good English war books (none better), that on my soul I feel semi-apologetic about mentioning another. A characteristically English reaction has begun against the truthfulness of good war books, which are said to malign our armies. An effort is being made to maintain that our soldiers, in addition to being heroes, were arch-angels. For myself I prefer them to have been what they were : men. I have no use at all for archangels, but a lot of use for men.

Well, I must mention yet one more fine English war book : Henry Williamson's *The Patriot's Progress*, illustrated by William Kermode. It is short, and it is not a novel. It contains very little concerning the supposed-to-be chief military (and civil) diversions : beer and light women. It is the account of the war-career of a plain, ordinary man, John Bullock, who entered the army with a dogged sense of duty, and left it minus a leg. The author has not drawn John Bullock as an individual. John Bullock is Everysoldier, and *Everysoldier* would have been an excellent title for the book.

The account is simple, and awful, absolutely awful. Its power lies in the descriptions, which have not been surpassed in any other war-book within my knowledge. I began by marking pages of terrific description. But I had to mark so many that I ceased to mark. I said : " Nothing could beat *that*, or

that or *that.*" I was wrong. Henry
Williamson was keeping resources in
reserve for the supreme attack in which
Everysoldier lost a leg. This description
(p. 169), quite brief, is a marvel of
inspired virtuosity. And it is as marvel-
lous psychologically as physically. In
fact when I had read it I said to myself:
" I ought to retire from the craft of
descriptive writing, for I am definitely
outclassed." No overt satire, sarcasm,
sardonic irony in the book. Yet it
amounts to a tremendous, an over-
whelming, an unanswerable indictment
of the institution of war—" the lordliest
life on earth ."

A word as to Mr. Kermode's pictures.
At first I resented them, for they are
very numerous and they cut into the
text, distracting the reader's attention.
But in the end they justified themselves
to me. For they are very good, and
just as much a part of the book as the
text itself. It would be as fair to say
that the text illustrates the pictures
as the pictures illustrates the text. The
two forms of expression are here, for
once, evenly complimentary. *The
Patriot's Progress* ought to have a large
sale.

Well, that was a generous bit of writing by
Arnold Bennett, a most sensitive and kindly
man both in his work and in his presence ; and
the suggestion of provincial ' vulgarity ', which
more than one biographer of Bennett has

suggested, is to my knowledge entirely pre-
sumptuous.

Now follows a second criticism, written to the
author by ' T. E. Lawrence ', a man later to
be misunderstood and even maligned ; but let
the reader judge.

>   18.3.30—21.3.30. Much interrupted.
                            338171 A/C Shaw
            T.E.S.   R.A.F. Mount Batten
                            Plymouth

Dear H.W.

I have been too long, perhaps, over
the Patriot's Progress : but after my
first reading of it everybody in the
Hut got hold of it, and I only saw it
again yesterday, when I read it for the
second time.

It is all right : that is the first thing
to say. To do a war-book is very hard
now, after all that has been written,
but yours survives as a thing of its
own. I heaved a great sigh of relief
when it was safely over. I like it all.

Your writing scope grows on me. This
book is a tapestry, a decoration : the
almost-null J.B. set against a marvel-
lous background. It is the most completely two-dimensional thing possible
—and on the other hand you give us
your cycle of novels (about yourself, I
dare say) which are as completely
three-dimensional, full of characters as
a Christmas Pudding of almonds,
with the background only occasional,

and only occasionally significant. I am
convinced, by both Tarka and the P.P.
that you have many other books to
write before you repeat yourself and
become a classic.

I sandwiched the P.P. between read-
ings of " Her Privates We ".* The P.P.
is natural man, making no great eyes
at his sudden crisis : whereas " Her
Privates We " shows the adventures
of Bourne, a queer dilettante, at 'grips
with normal man in abnormal circum-
stances. The two books complement
each other so well. Yours is the first
quite unsentimental war-book—except
for its last page, and nobody could have
resisted that kick of farewell. I should
have thought less well of you without
that touch of irony here and there.

The incidental beauties of the book
—the dew-drops on its leaves—are so
common as hardly to be seen. That, I
feel, is right in a book whose restraint
is so strong. You seem to be able to pen
a good phrase in simple words almost
as and when you please. You beat
Bunyan there, for he got to the end
of his P.P. without throwing in a
deliberately fine phrase. I noted with
pleasure

p. 5   The sun-flickers on the toppling
         wave.
p. 28   The winter : very, very good it

---

*By Frederick Manning. His book is a masterpiece. H.W.

is. An epitome of Salisbury Plain.

p. 39   That journey to the coast.

p. 40   Wriggling, shiny . . .

p. 53   Light ran and trembled

p. 58   Light-chinks wavered

p. 59   Dimming . . . does it dim ? I hesitated for two moments here.

p. 64   haze almost of powder

p. 73   in a vacuum . . .

p. 86   The nailed boots bit

p. 88   A fluttering butterfly of light

p. 104   dilated by every ruddy crash

p. 116   gangrenous light of dawn

p. 117   The broken skull is beautifully observed

p. 125   ribbed serpent's corpses . . . but isn't this almost too technical a picture ?

p. 129   The picture and metaphor of Ypres is superb.

p. 159   Puckering the water . . . superb: didn't need the toad's back, really.

p. 169   his v. trembling body was now large and alone.

p. 184   Rootlets of their minds growing in hope towards England.

If some unkind power forbade me to take interest in that little list I could make a second and a third list of delights. Craftsmanship like yours warms one, to meet.

I begin to suspect that you may be one of those comparatively rare authors who write best about people or things other than themselves. I hope so, because it is the sort that last longest, unless one is a very deep man, like Dostoievsky, and can keep on digging down into oneself. I hope you aren't that, because it means misery for the artist, and the two roads, happiness and misery, seem to be equally within our choice, and it's mere common sense to be happy.

Tarka and this P.P. are better than your novels, I think, because you get further outside the horrific convolutions of your brain in each. The objective, as somebody would properly say, which is the classic rather than the romantic manner.

I have enjoyed the P.P. very much. The Hut fellows say it isn't properly named, it being not a " bloody bind " like that Bunyan chap's stuff. " Bind " is a lovely word : mental constipation.

I sit in Mount Batten all day and sleep all night, very quietly content, but sweating every spare hour I get over old Odysseus, a new version of whose adventures I am producing (on a cash basis) for a very rich American. Hope he likes it better than I do— but the cash will be superb when it is all over.

All over will not be much before November next, I fear : but I shall run out before that and see you. I swear it. Does not your postcard address still live

in my breast pocket? (right breast,
alas: a pencil holds the honour of
my heart's pocket!)

My regards to Mrs. W. and the tod-
dlers, who have a long way to grow,
yet.

Yours

T. E. Shaw

FIRST PHASE

JOHN BULLOCK, a youth beloved by his parents, was a clerk in the City of London. Both his father and mother came of farming stock ; his grand-parents had come from the country to work in the new factories being put up everywhere during the young Queen Victoria's reign. Two generations away from the sun on the fields had changed ruddy faces to pale faces, but the father did not think of this. His chief concern was that his son should have a better life than he himself had had : this meant more money. So John became a clerk when he left the Council School, and his father was very proud of him. Every morning John Bullock went to London on a train that took twenty-two minutes to reach Cannon Street Station—unless it were foggy. Except in the hot summer the windows of the train were closed ; men and girls were sitting close together on the seats, seldom speaking. Puffing pipes, reading newspapers which formed the surface of their minds, wearing sombre clothes, usually shapeless, and hard bowler hats, the old and middle-aged men in the carriages were once like John Bullock. Although the thought was rarely,

if ever, expressed, these men believed that they
were of the finest race on earth, superior to all
foreigners. Twenty-two minutes up to the City
every morning, before nine o'clock : twenty-two
minutes down every evening, after six o'clock.
All of them working so that their wives and
families should eat and live ; some of them
thinking, at odd moments, of the sun on the
English fields, and dreaming of better days for
their children ; then reading their papers again,
in the smoky air of the shaking compartments,
with rare and scarcely-formed thought that their

way of life was inevitable, and that such conditions of fog, rush, negation of dreams, fatigue, semi-insecurity of their jobs, would remain until the end of the world. John Bullock was expected to arrive before nine o'clock every morning at his office near Cannon Street. He addressed envelopes, typed and copied letters in the press book, and nearly always did what the chief clerk told him. At one o'clock he went out to his dinner, which often he ate on London Bridge, watching the ships in the Pool of London, the human life on the wharves, and, in winter, the gulls screaming and soaring along the parapets. Sometimes he walked to St. Paul's, and opened the sandwiches his mother made for him on the steps ; or strolled to the fish-market by the Monument. Another haunt of his was in Gracechurch Street, where, beside a smoky church, was a garden with white-splashed paths and seats in plane-tree shade ; and pigeons which cats tried to catch, and sparrows which often were caught and borne away shrieking. When John heard the chirping shriek of the teeth-pierced sparrow he wanted to rescue the bird, but he did not act on his desire. Nor did any one of the many other quiet people resting and eating in the old churchyard, although only the aged or the destitute did not feel sorry for a dying sparrow. The summer of 1914 arose over the streets of London like any of the five other City summers John Bullock had known since leaving school at the age of fourteen years. It was hot in the streets, from which arose

the smell of solid-tyred motor-buses and the
dust-specks of horse traffic. One day towards the
end of July John Bullock felt very pleased with
life, for on the first of September he was going to
cycle down to the seaside, and begin his yearly
holiday of fourteen days, to which he looked
forward, and saved up for, all the rest of his year.
He would see the sun on the fields, and shining
on the sea ; he would hear band music at night
under the moon, and perhaps meet a girl who
would be as beautiful as the advertisement for
the Face Cream he had cut out of a sixpenny
magazine and pasted (with office paste) into his

pocket book. Fishing, his new white flannel trousers (5s. 11d., Aristos), sailing, pier, un-limited ices and ginger beer, no train every morning, the sun-flickers on the toppling wave—fragments of mental pictures of these and other happinesses made him content as he strolled back to the office, fag in mouth, hands in pockets. He passed a newspaper shop just as the owner was putting out a board with the contents bill in large black type—

TO HELL WITH SERVIA!

The paper was called *John Bull*. He forgot it immediately; but he heard the word Servia

again and again. Something about a bomb.
Everyone was talking of a bomb and Servia,
same old rubbish in the paper day after day. And
on August Bank Holiday John Bullock came
home and found his father reading to his mother
about the threatened invasion of Belgium, and
the mobilization of Russia and Germany. The
Serbian news was no longer rubbish. As the
August days went on the men in the train, who
usually would only look round their papers without speaking if one trod accidentally on a boot
and made apology, became more and more

genial ; to dare to try and sit down on a seat made for five and just holding four bulky forms was almost an act of friendship. In the London County Council Recreation Ground where he met his friends every evening " To hell with Servia !" had become " To hell with Germany !" Soon the extent of Germany's behaviour became known through the newspapers : the Germans were burning the Belgian villages, shooting old people and sticking bayonets through Belgian babies, raping the women during drunken orgies, and cutting off the limbs of children. Kitchener appealed for an Army of 100,000 men, and John hurried to enlist for " three years or the duration," anxious lest the war might end before he saw some of the fun. Everyone said the war would be over by Christmas, for the Russian Steamroller was rolling towards Berlin, and in France the Huns—as the Germans were now called—were losing all their men in mass attacks which always failed. This common knowledge was in every newspaper, and on everyone's lips. For hours John stood in a queue with other men, outside the door of the Recruiting Office. At last his turn came : off with collar, tie, shirt, and vest : boldly he spoke the words Ninety-nine, out of his chest unnaturally inflated. It was a nervous moment when, in a line with other men, he swore the Oath of Allegiance, holding a Bible very firmly between finger and thumb while a gentleman in uniform spoke words for him to repeat ; but by the time he got home the nervous

moment had become a proud moment, and he
had forgotten how he had mumbled the words
before other men. That afternoon he went up to
the office to say good-bye to the other chaps, and
to shake Old Smith, the head clerk, by the hand.
His place, of course, would be kept open for him,
he was informed by the Boss. Others had joined
up too; but young Walton, always rather
superior owing to his superior education at a
secondary school, was still there. He explained to
John, who felt grateful to him for speaking so
nicely to him, that as soon as the Firm could
spare him he would go too; and he mentioned
how many of his relations were with the Services,
one of them being a Captain in the Army Service

Corps. He would ask this captain cousin to keep
an eye on Bullock if he ran across him ; and
John left to go home feeling that he could look
anyone in the face. If only he had been in uniform, with a gun or a sword ! The next morning
he had to report to the Recruiting office at

nine a.m. At a quarter past eight he said good-
bye to his mother and father, hastily kissing his
mother, and, after hesitation, shaking his father's
hand. " You won't forget to keep your feet dry,
will you, dear," said his mother, and looked at
him with pride that hid her sadness. She wanted
to ask him to be sure not to forget his prayers ;

but, remaining silent, her heart began to ache. Perhaps he won't be needed out there at all, she thought, but will be kept for Home Defence. " Good-bye, Son ! " she clasped him, silently praying. " Good-bye, old man," said his father, smiling. "Write when you're not busy." "Righto. I don't expect there'll be much time, you know, but I'll keep you posted." " Thank you, dear," said mother, and wanted to clasp him once more, but he had opened the gate and was walking up the hill. " Well, mother, it's a righteous cause, and our Jack has acted like a man," said Dad, as the old folk turned back into the house again.

" Yes," said Mother, but she said no more, for a
void had come in her breast, that would remain
until her son came home again, and everything
was as before. A sergeant with a red-white-and-
blue rosette in his cap, very smartly dressed (his
tunic and trousers had been taken-in closer than
regulation fit by the depôt tailor) marched them
at noon from the recruiting office to the railway
station. Little boys marched by their sides, keeping better step than the recruits ; some old men
lifted their hats ; others when in groups, but
never singly, cheered ; one old lady waved out

of her window, crying shrilly, " Remember Belgium ! " In front of John Bullock marched a real gentleman—John knew he was that, because he wore a top-hat, like some of the rich directors of the other companies in the building, in whose near presence he had always felt subdued and inferior. Now he spoke to the tophatted gentleman with friendly ease, and even offered him a cigarette. Girls smiled at them, some of them saying, " Good luck ! " and at the railway station a crowd was gathered to cheer them away. With the others in his compartment John yelled and cheered, imagining himself smashing Huns with fat faces and pig-eyes, who ran away before the mighty cheers and thrilling trumpet calls of the Charge ! Before the end of the journey he was swearing like the seven other men, and had lost one shilling and fourpence at Nap played on a newspaper spread on knees— just as he had seen men playing sometimes on the 6.5 train home in the old days, when he had never dared to play, having been warned of the card evil by his mother when he had first gone to the City. People cheered and children waved to the men in the train ; more shouting and hat lifting when they marched, or rather ambled away from the station, a sort of broken human concertina moving along the street. They came to the barracks, and so entered the reality of a soldier's life. John Bullock was surprised, and slightly shocked, at the curt, almost rough, way the sergeants spoke to the recruits. After a meal of

bread and margarine, and a mug of tea that was too strong and too sweet, they were paraded in line and told off into squads, each under a man picked by an officer who appeared suddenly in the room. They were asked what experience they had ; and since the man with the top hat had used a shot gun on the marshes of the Thames, he was put in charge of John's squad—after his hat had been put aside, as ordered, on the shelf above his bed. The squad was marched to the Quartermaster's stores to draw palliasses and blankets and bed-boards, which they brought back to their room with its grey-painted walls. When each man had been given his numbered bed-place along the wall, the squad was paraded again and told that no passes would be issued that evening, but that they could go to the canteen and walk about inside the walls until nine-thirty, when they must be back in their room for Roll Call. Lights Out would be at ten o'clock. " Now then, when I say Dismiss, turn to the right, pause, and then break away. Party, 'Shun ! Spring to Attention there ! God damn it, you're like a lot of cripples. All right, fall out ! " Most of the squad had money in their pockets. John had tasted beer before, when cycling on Saturday evenings in the country, more a self-demonstration of his manhood and freedom than a refreshment ; and that evening, depressed by his surroundings and the loss of freedom, all so different from what he had imagined, he drank two pints in the canteen, and felt less lonely. The feeling of being more a man returned, and he pleased himself by swearing, a habit he had lost since his school days, and by truculent references to what he would do when he got hold of the Huns. This was the general feeling in the canteen until someone started singing, when their high spirits returned, and they cheered. When John went back to his room with a man he had chummed up with, a fight was going on, and several men were half drunk. The sergeant came in to call the roll when the bugles rang across the parade ground ; beer

bottles were hidden, orders were shouted. At ten
o'clock the lights went out as the bugles echoed
around the brick walls and windows ; and John
tried to sleep. He was too hot, sleeping in his
shirt and pants ; the brown blanket was harsh
round his neck, the square straw canvas-covered
palliasses were hard with the boards under them.
His neighbour coughed and spat on the floor ;
several men began to snore ; the traffic of lorries,
motor-buses and cars along the road outside the
barracks did not cease. He thought of his
mother's face, and wondered upon the future ;

the darkness pressed upon him. Just as he was trying to sleep a man down the room was sick, and someone else said " Christ ! " in a voice of disgust ; it was the sick man's neighbour. " What do you want to drink beer for ? " said another voice, "Lord Kitchener specially warned us against drink. We shan't win by drinks and cheering." To which the sick man, now recovered after the expulsion of the beer, replied with several oaths connected with salvation and private functions of the human body. Several men laughed, and the door of the sergeant's cubicle opened at the end of the room, and his voice said sternly, " Stop talking, and get down to it ! " Between one and two o'clock John Bullock fell asleep. He was awakened by the sergeant shouting in the room. Reveille had sounded two minutes before ; the sergeant was a Reservist, and a fortnight previously he had been a respectful and quiet publican in a west-country village. His voice was echoed by the Top-hatted Toff, as the recruit put in charge of Bullock's squad was already nicknamed. They fell in for physical exercises. After much confusion in numbering, and assorting odd numbers from even numbers, followed by more confusion upon opening ranks, they turned their heads left and right ; they bent backwards, forwards and sideways ; they went down on their hands, bending and straightening arms ; lifting legs, sagging and collapsing, groaning, blowing, and complaining. They dismissed for shaving and washing ; fell in for a

slice of cold fat bacon, bread, and thick-
sweetened tea. Afterwards they paraded for
squad drill, left turn, right turn, about turn, left
turn, on the right heel and the left toe, on the
left heel and the right toe, Christ a' mighty, they
were 'opeless as a lot of bleedin' sheep. Stand at
ease, stand easy, fer Gawd's sake. The corporal-
instructor was yellow-haired and pale-blue eyed ;
the fury of Indian sunshine beating on dusty
parade grounds was in his voice, gesticulations,
and bearing. Many muttered against him ; all
grumbled in heart or word ; all sweated and
hated the drill. They learned to salute, to jerk

their heads to right and left upon the orders of
Eyes Right ! and Eyes Left ! In the second week
they were marched to the Medical Officer's room
for inoculation. The left arm was bared, iodine
dabbed on by an orderly ; they approached the
officer ; their skin was gripped ; the needle was
jabbed in. One or two fainted, another was sick ;
the doctor punctured arms and injected anti-
typhoid serum at the rate of ninety an hour.
They were excused all parades for the rest of the
day. Some said it meant France at last, especially
as rifles, although of an antiquated pattern, had
been dished out. That afternoon John Bullock
shook with cold, his teeth chattered ; for two
hours he thought he was going to die, but at six
o'clock he felt better and went to have a wet in
the canteen. They still awaited uniforms. They
went for their first route march, still a human
concertina, but not ragged or broken or dis-
tended beyond itself. It was a long march, fifteen
miles. The rifle made his shoulders ache, and the
blisters broke inside his thin socks. His boots,
recently issued, were too big. He was a hundred
and ten miles away from home, and still hoped
for a week-end pass ; but the married men went
first, and then only five per cent. of the company.
John Bullock had been a soldier two months
when, one morning, all his room were stirred by
the rumour that uniforms were being dished out
—khaki uniforms, too, not the blue that many
battalions of Kitchener's Army were wearing.
" Latrine rumour, as usual," said the Corporal,

whose nickname of the Top-hatted Toff had long
been disused. Yet it was so ; and eagerly they
waited before the Quarter Bloke's store, for
tunics, trousers, puttees, and service caps. The
regimental badges and shoulder-titles were much
admired. Several attempted to pinch an extra
badge ; some succeeded. The rolling of puttees
was a mystery that few solved before a week.
The rolls opened like the gills of fishes ; they
were too thick round the ankle or too tight
round the calf. They groused about their puttees,
about their food, their parades, "Physical jerks,"
leave (or its remoteness) which they now called

" leaf." They hated with a fierce and sullen hate
the drill-instructors, often vowing that when
they got overseas a bullet would accidentally on
purpose one dark night. . . . John grew heavier,
more alert, his eyes brighter, his skin less like a
railway carriage window after a fog. One night
when the roll was being called, after he had
returned with his chum Ginger (not the original)
from the local cinema, the orderly sergeant read
out, " The following men will parade to-morrow
morning with kit-bags and such marching order
as they possess, for entrainment as reinforce-
ments to ——," and then followed a meaningless

place-name. Silent and tense they listened. Sounds of relaxation increased as name after name was read out. " No. 19023 Private John Bullock." Fine, leaving the blasted barracks at last ! Hurray ! The corporal called them to order sharply, and instant silence followed, with a reading of other names. The sergeant went away, they fell out, and what a hubbub and shouting with joy ! France next ! Anywhere, so long as they never saw the barracks again ! Imagination elated them with its mental pictures. After a merry and careless train-journey they got out at a bare-looking station, where many soldiers were

working or lounging, military vehicles with chalk dust on their grey-painted bodies and khaki-coloured hoods stood about, and military police-men with red-covered caps and brassards of M.F.P. on their arms. They marched out of a siding, watched by a tramp on the dusty wayside, who was binding his foot with a length of cast-off puttees. " Goin' to join us, dad ? " The tramp went on binding his feet as though oblivious of the scores of thousands of soldiers in the camp of the Great Plain. " Take that man's name for falling out without permission," cried another wag, in the mock-voice of an officer. The tramp did not even look up. They marched on, carrying kit-bags, and came to a camp of hundreds of bell-tents pitched in lines under the grey-green downs. Very soon it became for them what they called a God-forsaken spot, the last place God ever made, and other things. Twelve to a tent they slept ; there was no privacy. John Bullock was still shy about the outer functions of his body, and was unable to squat with the others on the latrines, which were dug close together near the washing place, a hundred dog-graves in the turf, and open to the sky. He used to wait until darkness, and then, if it were not too late, he would seek his own privy far from the camp and meditate under the stars on the strangeness of the world. He became ill, and reported sick, being marched to the M.O.'s tent by the orderly corporal. Two curt questions the M.O. asked, before saying " Number Nine " to the R.A.M.C.

sergeant behind him, and writing M. and D. against Bullock's name on the Sick Report. " Here, take this," ordered the sergeant, and gave Bullock a white pill nearly as big as a pea. One of the men complained of a pain, and he, too, was given Medicine and Duty—the medicine being a No. 9 pill and the duty being platoon drill, saluting, musketry drill, bayonet fighting practice, signalling with flags, extended order drill, and then dinner. After the dinner the man vomited, and was taken to the medical tent in a fever. Two days later his platoon learned that he had gone to hospital and been operated on for appendicitis. As for Bullock, he was cured of his headaches and his shyness, and even enjoyed the early morning visits to the Lats, as they were called by those men of the platoon who washed more regularly in the open wash-house of wooden

benches and galvanised iron bowls. They endured a winter of mud and cold and grousing discomfort in the camp on the Great Plain, and when the spring of 1915 came, and the beech clumps on the high downs became dark with leaves, they began to hope that they would leave the camp and go to France. " I hear that the Division is very pleased with us as a battalion," said the Colonel one night in the big marquee mess, where, his hands and face scrubbed, and hair plastered with water, John Bullock was on mess-waiter's fatigue. " The G.S.O.I. said he might be getting an idea of where we might be going before long." How John Bullock envied the mess waiters ! And the lovely food they had. And how noisy were the officers afterwards ; wrestling, singing songs, throwing things about, and rolling one of them in a carpet and lugging him to the incinerator. John wrote home about the fine feed he had had after the washing-up. Still they did not leave the camp on the Great Plain. From man to man passed all kinds of rumours—they were going to France to take part in the Big Push to Berlin ; they were going to Gallipoli—had not the C.O. recently worn a pair of light khaki-drill breeches ? ; they were being kept against a German invasion of the East Coast, where all the gun-platforms had been made in readiness before the War on concrete tennis courts and the roofs of German-owned hotels ; they were going to India ; to South Africa ; to Gibraltar ; Malta ; Japan ; nowhere. The summer waned into autumn, and still they went for route marches, carrying rifle and 150 rounds of ammunition in web pouches above their belts, water-bottle and haversack, en-trenching tool at the base of the spine, entrench-ing tool handle and bayonet in its leather sheath

at the left side, and pack containing a folded
great-coat. Long since had shoulders ceased to
ache at these weights of about fifty pounds, or
feet to swell, and few had blisters. Foot inspection was held after every route-march ; the skin
of their necks, faces, hands and wrists was brown,
their eyes clear ; they laughed and sang and
drank beer and groused. John Bullock went
home on leave three times in the year he had
been a soldier ; each time he was given a voucher
that enabled him to buy a return ticket for half
the price of a single fare. One day, soon after the

Daily Mail had printed the headline, *A Real British Victory at Last* above an account of the Battle of Loos that thrilled and gladdened millions of English people, a rumour rushed round the camp that shortly the tents were to be taken into store. The Break Through ! Huns on the run ! A wave of the 1914 excitement broke over the battalion ; songs were louder in the tent-lines, more beer was drunken on pay-night. Soon came the backwash, in the statement from the platoon sergeant, who got it from no less an authority than the Regimental Sergeant-Major

—a thin, upright, tough, elderly man, with a scarred face and clipped moustache, who dressed like an officer, was addressed as " Sir " by all the rank and file, but not saluted—that they were not going away, but huts were to be erected for the winter on the same camp. The grey rain drifted like smoke over the downs, over the rows of brown wooden huts. Streams of rust ran down the stove pipes ; the wind moaned across the chimneys as they sat there during the long winter evenings. " Three years or the duration " became an ironical phrase. Some of the men in

John Bullock's platoon went away to become
officers, others asked for transfer. When the
spring came, the spring of 1916, hope revived a
little with the lessening of the mud-sheets about
the dreary acres of hutments. Men began to talk
of the strength of the Allies and the decreasing
power of the Germans. " Wait until Kitchener's
Army goes out ! " they said. They cut their
regimental badge in the slope of the downs above
the camp ; digging away the turf and opening
the chalk to the sunlight of a thousand thousand
years ago. Other badges were cut by other regi-
ments ; they were seen for miles around. They
read of the Somme battles, and longed to be on
those other chalk slopes away from this bloody
awful plain. And when in the third August of the
war, steel helmets were issued to the battalion,
rumours grew numerous as the summer flies
about the incinerators—for there was much food
wasted in the camps ; scores of loaves, uncut
and half eaten, dixies full of potatoes, stew,
chunks of bacon were thrown away every day on
the heaps, for the civilians to take away in their
horse-butts, to feed the pigs with. All talked of
the great Somme victories. By next Christmas,
some said, the war will be over : Yes, and we
shall still be here in this bloody hole, said others.
Roll on, Duration ! Then came the blow, which
struck the Colonel hardest ; and shook the
second-in-command ; and made the company
commanders curse ; and fed-up the platoon
officers ; which made the R.S.M. secretly happy,

for he had been severely wounded in the Boer
War, and but for this War would have been in
civvy life with a pension, and he had no illusions
about active service ; and the sergeants, some of
them back from France, to argue whether it was
better to be stuck there in the mud where you
could get a pint, or to be stuck in the mud where
you couldn't ; and the private soldiers to grouse
at the way the troops were being messed about.
The news, that came from Brigade one morning
early in September, that the battalion would find
drafts to reinforce those of its battalions in the
field. Shortly afterwards the rank and file re-
joiced exceedingly, for when Battalion Orders
were read out one evening, it was learned that
twenty-five per cent. of the battalion would be
granted four days' leave immediately, to be
regarded as Draft Leave. Company commanders
were to detail officers to march the first parties to
the station at 6.30 a.m. on the morrow, with
haversack rations. There were songs and cheering in the canteen and in the huts that night,
which were increased, rather than abated, by
the rumours which had begun to trickle among
them about the awfulness of the Battle on the
Somme. Well, the sooner they were helping the
boys out there, the better ! Hurray ! John
Bullock felt strong and lusty in his nailed boots.
Roll on, Duration.

SECOND PHASE

Towards evening John Bullock, who had been strolling with his friend Ginger on the downs during the afternoon, went to his hut and began, with other men of his draft, to put together his equipment. He worked with a slow seriousness never experienced before. They had been excused all parades after mid-day ; the webbing of their equipment had been scrubbed and cleaned with khaki blanco until it looked cleaner and neater than when it had left the Army Ordnance Department at Pimlico. The brass buckles and tabs shone very bright. The iron ring of the entrenching handle was burnished to the gleam of silver, with the bayonet handle lock and guard, the point of the scabbard, and the tin-opener and spring of his jack-knife. The rifling of his short Lea-Enfield glimmered marvellously with the least film of oil. Even the soles of his draft boots had been blacked and polished. Outside the battalion orderly room, with its white-washed row of flints, by which the sentry of the Headquarters Guard with fixed bayonet paced regularly, a bugler appeared, and sounded the call for the Orderly Sergeant. Soon afterwards voices arose in some of the huts. Fall in the Draft ! Outside the company office ! Get a move on ! They began to quicken their movements. Tunics were straightened, buttons hastily touched to make sure once more that they were fastened, trousers reset again. Arms were crooked into the braces of heavy and pendulous equipment—the soldier's Christmas tree. Cartridge pouches, filled water-bottle, stuffed haversack, slung P.H. gas helmet, entrenching tool and handle, bayonet in scabbard, massive rectangular pack holding housewife, groundsheet, overcoat, spare underclothes, socks and the intimate odds of each man's property, these

linked and connected were bumped and heaved on the back, shaken into place, and held fastened by the broad web belt. Steel helmets, called tin hats, were lifted gingerly on to heads, and the chin straps adjusted. The chin strap made John Bullock feel very strong and soldierly. " Hon parade ! Come along there ! At the double ! " The Captain and his officers, his C.S.M., his C.Q.M.S., followed by the company orderly sergeant, and the platoon sergeants of each platoon in turn, inspected them. Afterwards they stood easy, while the Captain wished them good luck, saying how much he regretted not going with them : but he couldn't help himself. It was bad luck, but there it was, he supposed the Higher Authorities knew best. " And boys," he said, suddenly dropping the voice of an officer and speaking as one of themselves, " give the boche hell ! The sooner they're all killed, the sooner we'll have peace. And if the fat Hun ups with his hands and cries Kamerad !— a little habit of theirs after they've fired all their rounds—well you know what you were taught to do to the stuffed sacks on the bayonet fighting parades. Personally, I prefer pig-sticking, for you can at least eat a pig." They laughed. He felt he was popular : a temporary captain, before the War a bank clerk earning £110 a year : often he wished he was of the regular officer class, hence the reference to pig-sticking. " Draft ! Properly at ease everywhere ! Draft, 'shun ! Move to the right in fours ! Form fours ! Right ! By the left, quick march ! Carry on Sar'-Major ! " Lep-right, lep-right ! lep-right ! cried the C.S.M., and the hundred men—nearly half the company— marched across the worn parade ground to opposite the orderly room, where the R.S.M. was waiting by the drum-and-fife band. " B. Company Draft—at the halt—on the left—form platoon!" Four hundred men were in the battalion draft, drawn up one company behind the other ; A, B, C, and D. The rattle of drums and the thin colourless piping ceased. The R.S.M. called the Parade to attention. All present A. Company draft ? Present, sir ! All present B. Company draft ? Present, sir ! All present C. Company draft ? Present, sir ! All present D. Company draft ? Present, sir ! The R.S.M. turned about as though with an impersonal controlled fury ; marched to the orderly officer ; stamped himself to attention ; flung up his right arm in a rigid salute ; and barked out : " Draft all present, sir ! " " Thank you, Sar'-Major," murmured the Orderly Officer, returning his best salute. After inspection, " Parade, stand at ease ! Stand easy ! " They waited, talking in low voices. The orderly room door opened. The R.S.M. said to the Orderly Officer, in a voice of respectful confidence, " Adjutant coming, sir." "Parade, 'shun ! " Assuming something of the rigidity of the R.S.M., the Orderly Officer strode towards the Adjutant and reported the draft all present and correct. " Fall in the officers," said the Adjutant. The draft conducting officers, under a captain recently second-in-command of a company, took their places in front of their men. The Colonel, who had been watching through the Orderly Room window, opened the door and stepped out. The sentry presented arms, and the C.O. touched his cap with his gloved hand. " Par-ade ! 'SHUN ! " cried the Adjutant, and in his smartest, his stiffest walk, he went up to the C.O. and saluted almost as rigidly as the Orderly Officer had saluted him. After the inspection the Colonel stood the parade at ease, and spoke as follows :—" Men of the Blankshire Regiment ! You are about to go overseas to join one of your battalions in the field. I need hardly remind you of the traditions of the Regiment, and of its proud record in other wars, for all of you are familiar with them. Nor need I remind you of the purpose for which you have joined the Regiment, in this the greatest of wars the world has ever known. Our cause is righteous, and God will crown our efforts with Victory, of that no right-thinking man can doubt for a moment. Meanwhile, I am confident that each one of you will do his duty in the spirit that has made our nation the finest race on earth. I only wish I could come with you—but it has been decided otherwise. Men of the Blankshire Regiment ! I wish every one of you Good Luck ! " A man cheered, others followed, the N.C.O.'s and Warrant Officers tried half-heartedly to check them. Hip, hip, hurrah ! The lusty cheering was echoed around the huts enclosing the hollow square of the parade ground. Isolated groups of men by the distant huts cheered back, and wished they too were going with the draft. Headed by the drums and fifes, and led by C.O., Adjutant, and R.S.M., they went to the station, accompanied by the battalion mascot, a little

mongrel dog called Kaiser Bill, who had a choice of a thousand beds to sleep on at night, and a thousand hands to feed his dainty and affectionate face. Eight to a carriage. Packs and rifles on the racks and under the seats. Games of nap. Laughter, singing, fags. Looking out of the win-

dow and waving to every girl they saw. Towards
the coast the country became flat and un-
inhabited, with tidal creeks grown with reeds,
where herons, long since grown heedless of
trains of singing men, stood in the distance, or
flapped away into the sunset. The men became
quieter, and soon the plaintive songs which
expressed their gentler, inner selves were being
sung in the darkened carriages. Lines of houses,
grey and crowded ; small dim dots of lights in
line. The train halted, drew on, jolted to a halt
again. A searchlight swung around the sky,
wavered, and vanished. At last the train glided
into a shed with a high peaked roof, and stopped
alongside a very long platform lit by arc-lamps.
Sergeants' voices arose outside : All men to
remain in their carriages. Orders came for them
to fall in on the platform in fours ; then they
piled arms, and sat down, or remained standing
where they were, in fours. Whistles sounded,
engines blew off steam, and shunted ; the vast
shed enclosed busy platforms farther than sight.
John Bullock felt very small and lonely as he
leaned on the muzzle of his rifle. The distant
shouts and clankings of shunted trains in the
unreal light gave him, for the first time in two
years, a sense of being part of something that
was immensely inevitable and beyond human
control. What were they all doing there ? He
thought of his mother and father at home, and
of the parting at the station—not Waterloo, for
he had felt he could not endure to leave them on

the big, lonely, crowded platform, where on former leaves he had seen so many women crying and waving handkerchiefs. " Fall in on your Rifles, B. Company ! " He drew a deep breath. The Great Adventure had really begun ! They marched down the platform, under the high wooden sheds, and came out into the colder air of night. Another wait. Slowly moving forward. Boots clattering on the gangways. His turn. He was on board the transport.

The arc lamps glistened on the water heaving between the side of the boat and the wooden piles. It sucked and slapped down there. Farther along the quay many short squat guns stood ; someone was saying he had had a look at them, and they were all ripped and torn and gashed. Blimey, if solid steel got like that, what price. . . . Cranes were swinging waggons on board. Mules being pushed and pulled. Many voices of authority. Before he realised it the ship was gliding away from the quay. The wriggling shiny lines of the arc-lamps converged and multiplied on the dark water, the unutterably desolate dark water gliding wider between John Bullock and what, he now realised with a piercing anguish, was his life. England ! No cheering, no band music, no waving forest of girls' hands : all so different from what he had scarcely formulated in his mind. Cigarette points glowed and lost bright sparks in the freshening breeze. Men began walking about, hands in pockets. " B. Company draft, this way ! " cried his sergeant.

They stumbled below, were allotted a place each on a lower, covered deck. Life belts were handed out, and fixed round chests. Some started sparring in fun. Chums wandered on the upper deck again. Quicker throbbing engines. Greenish-

brilliant light flashing on the right side of ship. Blimey! They shut their eyes. The searchlight swung over the water. The ship throbbed on, leaving spreading white wake. Dots and dashes of light in the darkness. Spy! Men thronging starboard rails. Soon the order " All pipes and cigarettes out!" Escorting destroyer had signalled " Submarines," someone told John Bullock, and " Submarines," John Bullock hastened to tell his neighbour. The wind freshened. The ship pitched and rolled. Many were sick. Soon after

daylight they were off Havre in sunlight. Biscuits, nearly as large as dog biscuits, and bully beef for breakfast, and water. Pilot boat approached : small man in peaked cap. " Give 'em *It's a long way to Tipperary* when you land— they haven't heard it before," he shouted, and the ship roared with laughter. They disembarked

on a quay piled house-high with rolls of barbed
wire hundreds of yards long and wide as a street
of houses. Listless German prisoners working
among them. Little boys begging, " Souvenir,
Bully Biff ! Tommy, old boy, give me cigarette,"
and using soldier-oaths beside the marching men.
Through the town, tramlines, uphill, ugly French
girls, Chocolat Menier in blue, wooden sabots,
old women in black, lounging soldiers. To the
Rest Camp. Khaki everywhere. Military police
with revolvers. Greenish-grey English motor
cars making constant dust. A hell of a march to

the Rest Camp. Dust, sweat, blistered feet on the pavé roads. They arrived at last. Thousands of dingy bell-tents. Dust. No grass. Enclosed in barbed wire. More military police with revolvers by the gateway. Speed 6 m.p.h. for all motor traffic. Twelve in a tent. Christ, what a bloody hole. Worse than the Plain. Roll on, Duration! Y.M.C.A. hut a godsend. Crowded, clamouring, smoky. John Bullock looked at the women waiting outside, repelled, yet fascinated. French girls so pretty, 'struth! These were fat and painted. " Ask for a pass, Tommee! " they wheedled.

" Ma chambre is ver' close 'ere ! " Little boys
were there, too, saying, " Jigajig my sister for
ten francs, Tommee ? " and when the soldiers
grinned, " You dirty little bastards," the little
boys replied imperturbably, almost formally,
with the authentic London retorts. John Bullock
returned to the Y.M.C.A. and wrote a letter to
his mother, saying he was enjoying himself ; that
the crossing had been rough, but he wasn't very
sick. France very interesting country, but he
mustn't say where he was. After dinner, feeling
the Romance of War, he wrote again to his

father, telling him it would be over by Christmas and ending up with a graphic description made of unconsciously borrowed newspaper accounts, of the sullen mutter of the guns bombarding in the distance, etc., etc. Actually the only sullen mutter he could hear was the lumps of bully beef stew being bombarded by the gastric juices of his belly. Two days in the Rest Camp fed them up to the teeth. Rumours came as frequently as the swirling dust between the tent lines; rumours—the imaginative essence of men enclosed and dominated in herds like cattle. At evening they marched down the hill again, singing, *There's a Long Long Trail a-Winding*. The moon shone in the sky, and most of them were happy, feeling confidence in themselves to face what other men had faced and survived. Every man thought secretly, I cannot be killed. The little boys walked beside them begging ; the old Froggies looked on with the least interest. They were marched into a siding strewn with paper and horse droppings. There they piled arms, and fell out, no man being allowed to leave unless for the latrines. Night deepened. The station lights

were paler and thinner than the coppery arc-lamps of Southampton docks. Greatcoats were put on. After waiting four hours they unpiled arms and were marched to a long grey troop-train, consisting of first-class carriages for the officers and rectangular wooden trucks painted *Hommes* 40 *Chevaux* (*en long*) 8 in white letters. There were wooden forms inside, but only enough for about half the men in each covered truck. Until midnight the men in John Bullock's truck talked, sang, smoked, drank, and ate. The train rolled slowly, with many stops and pauses. Its whistle was strange to his ears. It always whistled after a toot on the guard's horn, which sounded like a toy trumpet out of a Christmas cracker. The wheels ground the rails, and jolted regularly, slowly. For hours he tried to sleep, while curled like a distorted letter Z on boots and equipment and rifles, and between restless legs, while the wooden floor sent every grinding jolt and thump into his head. He was semi-conscious of sight and place, he awoke with a sour mouth, he dozed again ; and with the others yawned and shivered, hands in pockets, on his feet to watch the cold grey indifferent light of dawn. Poplars lined the railway, and, soon after sunrise, John Bullock saw many bully beef tins lying all along the permanent way. Some old and rusty, most of them blue, or with red and yellow labels curling on them. Men began to breakfast—*clink, clanger !* Other tins joined the continuous scatter lying there. More halts. Men got down and

were ordered to get back by sergeants. One came
back with daisies in his hand. " What's the
'urry ? Anyone would think there wasn't a war
on by all you chaps sitting there. Well, no 'urry,
so I'll go by train ; otherwise I'd walk up to say
'ow-de-do to Jerry." Already the attitude towards the enemy of both officers and men had
changed. The grey-clad German prisoners at the
base had been treated exactly as other soldiers
were treated : the enemy had become Fritz or
Jerry to John Bullock and his truck, who had
readily absorbed the attitude of the old soldiers

they had met. To the officers he had become tolerantly the old Hun and the Boche, nicknames which, for them at least, had lost the contempt and hatred of their inception. After breakfast many men were squatting on the foot-boards, hanging on like monkeys. A group of black clad women laughed shrilly in a far field and waved. Cheering broke out along the slow grey length of the train. " Blimey ! talk about Adam and Eve ! What hopes ! " " I wouldn't mind one of them pushers outside the Rest Camp now!" "'Ere, you ain't put no penny in the slot, sergeant ! " They were full happy now, for the sun was shining. John Bullock began to enjoy the experience. He lit another fag and skated the match through the open doors as in boyhood he had skated cigarette cards coming along the street home from school. This was the life ! On and on puffed the train, halting and dragging on, halting and jolting forward. They had long since ceased to look for signs of war. At first every broken down barn in the fields had been pointed out by the more excitable ; but when evening came all were lying or sitting on form or floor. " They've forgotten there's a war on." " Let's get out and push." " Crikey, couldn't I do with a pint of mild and bitter now." During one of the long halts John Bullock heard something that, immediately its significance was realised, brought all in the truck to their feet. They listened. A sound like very distant thunder, so slight that some doubted a sound at all. " Shut up, Ginger !

Listen ! " Ah ! That time there was no mistake.
All heard it. Another distant boom : others
filling the mellow evening air. Soon they had
resumed their former indifference, except the
few like John Bullock who were alert for further
sensations. Soon the air was shivering with distant reverberations. An aeroplane roared over
the jolting train. They saw a road where hundreds
of lorries were drawn up. Then a field of tents,
and picket lines with thousands of horses. The
cavalry ! Something expected ! But the cavalry
had been there for more than a year. More soldiers, lorries, waggons. Everywhere thick with
soldiers. An immense dump of shells piled one on
another, and hillocks of things like footballs with
an iron rod sticking out of each. Dust floated
over the roads. Lines of houses, some with
broken roofs. Lines of mules being led to water.
Another halt. " Pass it down—No man to leave
his truck without permission." The order was
shouted down from truck to truck. After a wait
of three hours the train went slowly forward, and
stopped in a station. They detrained there.
Formed up in fours. Stood easy. Waited another
half-an-hour. Marched away. John Bullock over-
heard an officer telling the sergeant that ap-
parently no one knew anything about them, or
where they were to go. After a night in a row of
houses—sleeping on floors, windows broken and
doors missing, paper stripped off walls and
innumerable initials, dates, regimental names
and badges written and drawn on the dirty

plaster—they marched up the line. It was rumoured that they were going to join a battalion in the trenches. The road was pavé in the middle, dusty at each side above ditches. A military policeman stood at a crossroads, directing traffic. They marched through a village where peasants stood and watched them, and children begged for "Biskeets and booly biff." Brick walls were chipped and pitted curiously : many tiles were off, and one roof fallen right in. Soldiers with caps on backs of heads stood before a corner house by a big notice-board with names

and directing arrows. They had glasses of beer in their hands. The draft cheered. " Just out, chum ? " " Yes. What's it like ? Are we going to attack ? Is this the Somme ? " " No, chum. It's a picnic up there. No need for any wind." After an hour they fell out on the right side of the road for ten minutes' halt. They marched on, with box respirators at the Alert, slung round the chest, and the flap undone. The guns were now loud in front somewhere. Light ran and trembled, flashed and quivered before them. They came to another village, whose broken walls they could

see against the darkening summer sky. A growling, droning sound grew louder and deeper ; and it seemed very near. A ruddy fan of light arose and soon afterwards a heavy crash. Most of them ducked. John Bullock's heart beat faster and he straightened his tin hat. More droning, buzzing downward curving sounds ; the uprising glares, the *womp*, *womp* of the exploding shells. They halted and were anxious. Those in front shuffled on. Then the whispered order. " Lead on, in single file. Sergeant Smith, follow with your two sections at fifty paces interval. Absolute silence."

They walked on warily. A terrific blast of light, a terrific clapping shock, and a vast hissing diminishing overhead. Someone cried out, all were shaken. The power and terror of a gun firing had never been imagined. There was a battery of 6-inch howitzers behind a farmhouse, firing slow harassing fire on the back-areas of the German lines, for this was the hour the horse transports brought up the rations to the battalion dumps. John Bullock filed on, often halting and bumping into the man in front. Other shells came droning with coarse downward furrow; ruddy glares; bursting with rending metallic crashes. John Bullock sweated and felt the New Testament in the tunic pocket over his heart— gift of the padre before the draft left the camp on the Great Plain. They passed a G.S. waggon, which was halted, its driver rapidly unloading boxes and tins. A match flared; a cigarette puffed. " For God's sake put that light out ! " The cigarette glowed, a voice growled. " Don't get the ———— wind up, chum ! " " Are they near ? " " 'Oo ? " " The Germans ? " " About a mile." " What's it like up there ? " " Cushy." Onwards again. They left the road and trod warily over an uneven field. " Mind that shell-hole ! Pass it down," was whispered, spoken casually, hissed with tension, carefully passed on, ignored. Ruins of walls, a stump of a church, rising and falling white lights on the near horizon. Shuffling on again. " Mind the wire ! " a voice saying by John Bullock's knee. " Jump

down. Steady. Take my hand." He scrambled
down and was in a narrow communication
trench zigzagging through the fallen and standing ruins of houses. Their boots clumped on
wooden duck-boards. After many more halts
they came to the Support Trench. This, like the
communication trench, was revetted with rusty
sheets of corrugated iron or expanded metal held
close to the sides by wooden posts. Lights
glimmered through holes and chinks under the
eastern parapet, which was thrown into a
wavering but perpetual silhouette by the lights

rising and falling in white curves some way in front. Crack ! They ducked. The sound was loud and sharp as the crack of an Australian stock-whip heard on the music halls—a German bullet passing twenty feet over their heads. A voice muffled, and yet very near, sounded by John Bullock's shoulder. " How many men, Sar'-Major ? " " Forty-seven, sir, including two ser-geants, three corporals, and five lance-corporals, sir. I've the nominal roll here, sir." A triangle of light appeared by his shoulder, which the figure of the C.S.M. partly filled. Within the small dug-out John Bullock saw an officer sitting at a table, a whiskey bottle open before him. Another officer was lying asleep fully dressed beside him, on a bed made of wire-netting nailed to a low wooden frame. " Right ho, Sar'-Major. I'll be out in a moment." " Very good, sir." The army blanket dropped again, and the light-chinks wavered until it hung still. John Bullock enjoyed his first night in the trenches. Silently, ceaselessly, the white-stalked flares rose in front over the flat mysterious ground. Bullets piped and moaned away overhead, or clacked over the trench. Shells scored the high immense darkness over the new and thrilling world, droning away into remoteness. They worked on the parapet, filling sandbags and laying them header-and-stretcher in the low and uneven places. About three o'clock in the morning, according to the luminous wristlet watch his father had given him, John Bullock crept under the gas-blanket of the cubby-hole he shared with six other men, and pulling his woollen balaclava helmet over his head, tried to sleep.

He was awakened by a voice crying in the blanket-doorway of the low box-like shelter. " Stand to ! " Outside the order was being repeated. " Pass the word down, Stand to ! " They crawled out of the dug-out into the trench, shivering, adjusting tin-hats, removing old footless socks from rifle-bolts. The white lights rose and glimmered, crossed and interwove, sank slowly and dropped. Wanly the vapour shifted

with the ghost of light. *Pop-pop-pop*—pause—
crack-crack-crack—*pop-pop-pop*— pss — pss — A
German machine gun traversing in front. The
faster clatter of a Lewis gun replied from the
English front line, two hundred yards away.
Each man in the support line fixed his bayonet,
stood his rifle against the parapet, and then,
stamping feet, swinging arms, or hands in
pockets, awaited the sergeant with the rum. He
came as the lights grew thinner and scarcer in
the cold and stagnant air of a field dawn, when
the first aeroplanes began to cross the lines,
unseen and just audible in the dimming night.
The sergeant smiled as he dipped the small
spoon into his canteen, and held it out filled with
brown rum towards an open mouth. " Stuff to
give the troops," said John Bullock's chum,
gasping, smacking his lips. Flame filled the
throat, spread warm in the belly. The sky grew
grey, the last light faintly hissed up over Noman's-land. " Pass the word down, Stand
down ! " Bayonets were unfixed and sheathed.
One man in every six was told off as sentry. The
others crept into their cubby-holes to sleep.
Cleaned their rifles, pulling an old sock, with
toes cut off, over the bolt. Shaved in a mouthful
of water in their canteens. Breakfast came up
three hours after sunrise—one-third of a very
small loaf, stuck with sugar and tea leaves ; half-
a-canteen of sugared tea ; a slice of cold bacon
congealed in blackish-brown fat. The tea tasted
of chloride of lime. After three days in support,

the Company went into the front line. The night was clear and starry. They filed past the waiting men, who were going out that night to billets six miles behind the lines. Sentry groups of three men were told off into Nos. 1, 2, and 3; No. 1 was up for the first hour. Trench stores were handed over; officers passed up and down the fire bays, explaining what work was being done, the position of wire-gaps; what patrols went out, and where. The two company commanders happened to stand near John Bullock, who was a No. 1 sentry staring with rigid alertness out over the pallid greenish-haze of Noman's-land. His own officer, a clean-shaven youth of twenty who spoke like a man of forty; and the other, a middle-aged man with spectacles and a mild manner when speaking to the men, who had nicknamed him The Nurse. John Bullock heard The Nurse say:—" The parapet is a bit low here; they pooped off eleven oil-drums before we took over, and ever since they've had a fixed rifle firing on it. We lost a man there last night, walking up Plum Alley. Bounding Bertha's the minnie; the emplacement is about ten yards

left of Three Pollards by a ditch—here on the map "—A wan circle of light played on the trench map held by Captain Shanks of his own company. " But we haven't asked the gunners to strafe it, as we've only got 4-inch stuff, and it's useless ; and the Old Hun retaliates for hours afterwards." " Well, come and have a final spot. Any rumours about going South ? " " Yes, but mostly from the latrine. Brigade's heard nothing." They moved away. John Bullock knew that going South meant the Somme, where the battalion had attacked on July the first, at a place called La Boiselle. The survivors did not speak of it, except indirectly, by reference. Once when John Bullock had asked an old sweat what it was like, the old soldier—he had been out since May, 1915—had replied, " Bloody hell, mate," and said nothing more.

When the corporal came round, he asked John Bullock what the two officers had been talking about. " Going South, eh ? " After telling him about the gas gong, what part of Jerry's parapet to watch, and not to fire until he got an order from the officer as a patrol was out, the corporal went away. That night in billets, six miles away in the village the draft had marched through on their way up, The Nurse got the rumour that the battalion was shortly going South again.   It arrived via John Bullock, the corporal, a sapper sergeant, a ration fatigue party, two limber drivers of the battalion transport, the transport sergeant, an officer's groom, " C " Company's

officers' mess cook, and The Nurse's batman.
" Pass it on. No. 2 sentry's up." John Bullock
crept into a dug-out, and smoked a cigarette
before trying to sleep. A candle guttered on a
rusty German bayonet stuck into the earth wall.
He blew it out and lay down. Something heavy
walked over his face. Ugh! It drew a cold,
slightly rough line after it. Green points flicked
and reappeared with rustlings and sounds of
scratching. He struck a match, held the flame to
the bare bayonet handle, while a rat sat up in the
corner, eating the stump of the candle. The
sector was quiet, only one or two men being
killed by sniper or whizz-bang or oil-drum during a company tour of three days, and the
corpses were carried on stretchers and buried in
ground consecrated by the chaplain of a former
division. Thus the rats were middle-sized, eaters
of candles when they found them, and moder-
ately afraid of a man. The German lights were
brighter than the British lights, and they were
more numerous. On the second night John
Bullock was ordered over the sandbags with a
wiring party, and another man had to carry a
wooden knife-rest on a pole over the uneven
ground, and through a gap in the further side of
the tangle of English wire supported in its
bramble-maze by screw-pickets of iron. One
knife-edge support was set on the ground ; the
other was placed as far as the coils of wire con-
necting them would pull out. He worked in a hot
tremble of unreality, and stood stiff and agonised

while an enemy light *whiss-sshh-ed* out of the ground very near him, and broke into the white, soft, downward dilating radiance that cast a greenish haze almost of powder on everything. Hissing it fell, fizzling on the ground, leaving utter darkness and daze, and a dull red molten blob, slowly darkening inside the eyeballs. "They can't see you if you keep frozen," said the voice of the Captain near him, after one such moment of terror. "All you men of the draft are doing very well," he declared casually, before feeling his way forward with the great stick he always

carried. John Bullock felt that he loved the Captain ; he tried not to flinch every time a light *whiss-sshh-ed* upwards ; tried not to imagine never, never seeing his mother again ; and when, the wiring being finished without a casualty, the order to return was loudly whispered, he almost regretted that he could no longer walk about almost a free man. No more did he duck when, standing on parapet or parados, a bullet cracked by his head, sometimes making his ears ring as though it had clipped the rim of his tin hat. And after a comfortable rear and meditation in a shell-hole where no one else had visited, he

returned thinking that the War was fine. Contentment spread into the next day ; and when
the letters arrived, brought by the post corporal
to the Company head-quarter dug-out from
battalion head-quarters, John Bullock was hap-
pier than he had been for months. He read two
letters from Mum and Dad, many times, study-
ing and cherishing even the envelopes. In the
afternoon rain began to fall steadily, washing
the wooden slats of the trench-boards outside
the dug-outs. He smoked until his tongue was
tired, but still it rained. Drops began to drip
from the sand-bagged roof. Towards evening the

wind arose, and the rain lashed the greying
monotony of the flat weed-grown field, although
none thought of it as a field—through which the
trench wandered and zigzagged, and in places
returned upon itself. Stand-to was cold and long-
drawn, with wet down the neck, round the cuffs,
and very soon on the thighs and belly ; but
endurable by the thought of warm lighted billets
and parcels after the relief that night. The rain-
streaks shone with the flares ; and while he was
crouching on the fire-step, looking out into the
cold nothingness of Noman's-land, he was

shocked by a sudden shriek, a ruddy glare, an instant sharp crash, hard stinging spurts of earth in the blinded face. Another. Another. Another. Ringing ear-drums, and uncrouching from under the sand-bagged parapet, his eyes unblurring, John Bullock saw the same scene, the hanging wavering light-shadows, the rain-streaks and the gleams of helmets, but confused by the glare within his skull. " Are you all right," someone was calling. No one had been hit. They waited, but no more whizz-bangs arrived. " Jerry's now cooking his sausages for supper," said the sergeant cheerfully, as he thought of billets. The rain fell. They waited, many with eyes shut in half-sleep ; even some of the sentries. While John Bullock squatted in his shelter, waterproof cape over shoulders, the sky leapt alight over the parados, and soon a thundering roar was rolling around the quivering night. He scrambled out past the wet and heavy blanket to watch the bombardment of the enemy line on the right. The noise and the light passed through him, emptying his body of himself, and leaving a vacancy of incoherence, excitement and under- lying fear. Standing up, gripping his rifle and looking out over Noman's-land, he realised men flinging themselves against the parapet. The ruddy stabs and thudding reports of rifles. The clicking of rifle bolts. The louder reports of Verey pistols. The crackling of rapid fire swept down upon them. Every man fired blindly into the flame-jagged darkness. German bullets

swished and cracked and thudded, as though bursting, into the parapet of sand-bags. The night was a tempest of fire. Every soldier, every broken tree-stump, every stake and picket out in front, had innumerable shadows blending and quivering, dissolving and recasting themselves elsewhere in sharp outline, dissolving again as new flares, new sprays of flares, hissed and popped and bloomed over the trench. A constellation of golden stars broke above Noman's-land, followed by rocket-showers of red and green fire-balls. Soon the shriek and flash of whizz-bangs. The heavy rending crash of five-nines. The upper crack and clang of shrapnel with its grey smoke, luminous and drifting. Behind John Bullock's head the sky was leaping with light. The British shells rushed overhead with the noise of engines blowing off steam in

Cannon Street Station. The German trench was marked by vast red winking of shrapnel, the flamy fans of the heavier shells. And the bright rain, sometimes slanted and flung crooked, sometimes vanishing in steam, was unfelt but realised by John Bullock only by a remote sense beyond

himself. When the night became normal again, with the rattle of rifles and machine guns far away in the dim north towards the Ypres Salient, his limbs were trembling. He felt no fear. He was exhilarated to be alive. " Did they attack ? " he asked the sergeant. The sergeant laughed. He too was exhilarated to be alive. " Wind up, laddie." Two men had been hit. Not long afterwards voices and the noise of feet on the trench-boards. The relief was filing in. John Bullock felt sorry for them, having to spend three days in the rain. They did not seem to care. During the five-minute wind-up, they had been waiting in the communication trench known as Plum Alley. They brought the news that Jerry ·had been raided by the next division. " They copped it, too." " A " Company commander, Captain Shanks, handed over to " D " Company in about a quarter of the time The Nurse had handed over to him ; and with the rest of " A " Company John Bullock walked away, often bumping into other men and scraping his pack against the sides of the deep Plum Alley, while the shadows of his helmet rose and sank on the wet clay weaker and dimmer, until they had left the pop of rifles far behind. They climbed out of the communication trench, and filed across fields, stumbling, losing touch, and waiting at the head of the Company. Men grumbled and swore : another of the captain's short-cuts. All right for 'im, with only a stick and a revolver and a haver-sack with a bottle of whiskey in it : what about

full marching order with rifle, etc., etc. Some of
them who had fallen in shell-holes and were
double-weighted with water threw away clips of
cartridges ; others were so tired—for they had
had little sleep or rest while in the line—that
they dropped their private sand-bags of coke,
precious fire-buckets, which, when seen, were
picked up by old soldiers following. After three
hours they found the road, and closing up, fell
into step. Soon a song was raised by the platoon
mouth-organist ; but it faded away. The sergeants shouted, " Come on, boys, keep locked up.

By the right ! It ain't far. Come on, there, lef'
right ! lef' right ! " They passed the zone of the
howitzers, and the sixty-pounders. Lorries
crawled past them. At last, after marching in a
vacuum from the feet upwards, they reached
billets, and were told off in accordance with the
numbers painted by the dilapidated door. Hot
tea with rum in it was dished out by grimy-faced
cooks. " That's right, boys, get it down, there's
good lads." After swallowing a quarter of a canteen of the hot and sickly drink, John Bullock
began to laugh and to tell his chum Ginger that

he felt quite blotto, old boy, absolutely blotto, and who cared a damn for what bloody well happened, etc. Their billet was in a barn, with cracked and broken walls stuffed with straw and sand-bags. Straw on the floor was pressed down, damp, muddy. Candles flickered beside cast-off boots, sodden packs, red cigarette spots. A bit of all right. Sleep, sleep, sleep, O lovely warmth and comfort, sleep until nine next morning, breakfast, no fatigues, sleep, sleep—ha, ha, blotto, he was the boy, rum was the stuff to give the troops. Good-night, Ginger, old man. In the morning,

after a leisurely breakfast—tea tasting of bully
beef and biscuit stew (" it's warm and wet, any
old how "), damp bread and congealed bacon ;
jam, plum and apple, P.B.I., for the use of—
they cleaned up. A soldier's best friend is his
rifle. 'Oos got a buckshee bit of four by two ?
Some bleeder's pinched my bleedin' pull-through.
No matter, I'll win the first one I see. Puttees
scraped, rifles oiled, equipment put out in sun,
they began itchycooing themselves. Many were
crummy. Crack ! that was a big 'un, Ginger !
John Bullock had felt an occasional stinging itch

on his belly and ribs and privates, and searching
he discovered a grey crawling insect, with a black
speck in its middle, in the crutch of his trousers.
Transfixing it with a pin, he watched with satisfaction as it kicked and cracked and slowly grew
smoky red in a candle flame ; until the blackened
pin suddenly burnt his fingers. Power was in the
sun ; they were happy, caps on backs of heads,
shoulders and arms easy and free. In the afternoon there was a foot inspection : again they
were amicably warned by the casual Captain
Shanks that it was a court-martial offence to

develop the swelled red tomato-like inflamma-
tion known as trench feet, that used to keep men
on light duty or even send them down to the
base. No good any more, boys; the game's
rumbled. Every man must rub his feet with
whale oil before going up the line, daily while in
the line, and when out of the line. Afterwards an
inspection of box-respirators and rifles, then a
parade for baths. Fatigue order, with respirators. They marched along, whistling and singing,
to the brasserie, and undressed in a hop loft.
Each man carrying his underclothes under an

arm, they hopped, naked and crooked and tense
in the cold air, playing jokes on one another, to
the shed where they handed over the smelly
woollen bundles. Then clutching their grey,
soiled little towels, they loped with exaggerated
shivering into the cavernous room where stood

the mash tubs, around which mounting forms
had been erected by the Royal Engineers. Six
men to a steaming tub which looked like the
sawn-off base of a big cask. The two inevitable
jokes—(1) Blimey, boys, I've always dreamed of
swimming in a brewery . . . and, (2) the joke

about the French beer, which was generally reckoned to be what it resembled, having some body in it at last . . . Pass the soap, Ginger, 'strewth, never knew you was so fond of it. Look at Nosey Bullock, crikey what a pair, 'is name shouldn't 'ave been Bullock, but . . . They wallowed in the dark tub, while a sapper stoked the furnace in the corner, and the chinks in the roof were blurred bright. Come on, out of it : get a bloody move on : there's more than you in the Bee Eee Eff ! Loath to lose the blessing of hot water, they ignored the bespectacled lance-jack below. Aow ! The sinking water was sucked away under the legs, and oogh ! cold gushed out of the tap. They hopped out, laughing by the time their feet slapped on the ground. Clean vest and drawers of thick pinkish wool, and grey shirt and socks were handed to each man. They dressed and fell in on the right of the road outside the brasserie, where some German prisoners were working, scraping the blackish mud into the gutters. Some wore civilian clothes, others the field-grey uniforms in which they had come down to the barbed - wire cages ; all had circles of bright blue cloth sewn into spaces cut into trousers and jackets. John Bullock stared at them as though they had not been men ; and was called out of his half-reverie by the voice of the sergeant shouting : " Fall in on your marker. By'r right. Stop talking ! " When they got back to billets tea was waiting for them in the big blackened dixies. Pay parade after tea:—waiting outside the Company office door: name called by C.Q.M.S.: stepping in smartly, saluting. Officer signing the slight brown-covered pay-book, handing it back with a five-franc note in it. One pace back, another salute ignored by hatless

subaltern holding out his wrist-watch'd hand for next man's book: and then about turn, smart steps to the door: relaxation. With his chum, the red-faced youth called Ginger, John Bullock went to find an estaminet marked up with the leaning, irregular letters—

EEGS
& CHIPS

Three days in billets, three in reserve half-shattered farms on day and night fatigues, three in support, three in the line. Raining, raining, raining, always bloody well raining was often ironically sung to the hymn tune of *Holy, Holy, Holy, Lord God Almighty*. They learned more or less how the war was going on by the three-days-old newspapers, from home, sent by the post. Their letters sent home declared that most of them were in the pink. And one evening the rumour spread that the Division was being relieved; and that night the Jocks filed into the trench instead of the men of " D " Company. The next day the battalion marched away from billets, south-west into country where the poplar trees were straight and regular, the harvest fields unpitted, and at night the gun flashes were slight and almost forgotten. They were for it ! Down to the Somme again. Well, it was a good war in billets at night. Roll on, Duration !

THIRD PHASE

THE white dust was on every boot and puttee.
The grey mud was cracked in the ditches. By the
farm houses stood the harvest wains with their
high wheels, half-rotten. Sometimes an old man,
veteran of 1870, about the farm ; and many ugly
women. They did not like the English soldiers,
who took their straw and their swedes, scrounged
their wood and searched for eggs, and were not
above milking their cows and winning their hens.
Every theft was exploited by the peasants, who
made extravagant and perpetual claims. Many

hated the soldiers ; the quantities of tobacco and bully beef and the dumps of dung left behind by the transport lines were commonplace. C'est la guerre. Les Anglais were on their land : the peasants wanted to be left alone to their life work. Twelve to fifteen miles a day the Division marched : first one brigade leading, then another, then the third. It was a proud moment for John Bullock when his company led the battalion, and his battalion led his brigade, at 8 a.m. one morning, from the oak woods where they had put up their bivvies the night before. Red and yellow were the woods they marched by, so peaceful and silent under the sun of early morning. Their nailed boots bit the worn, grey road. Sprawling midday rest in the fields above the sunken valley road, while red-tabbed officers in long shiny brown boots and spurs cantered past on the stubble, the larks rising before them. But the sunshine ceased ; and it rained, and rained, and rained. On the sixth day they rested, with morning inspection of field dressings, rifles, iron rations—a pound tin of bully beef, and six biscuits in a linen bag, most of them being broken and even powdered—followed by gas drill by numbers. In the afternoon they were told to rest, and to get as much sleep as they could, in preparation for the night march. Company Parade at 19$\frac{1}{2}$ hours. Head of battalion to pass a certain point in a certain road (map reference given to adjutant personally by the brigade major) at a certain time. " And if anyone asks

you what battalion, regiment or division you
belong to," said Captain Shanks before dis-
missing the parade, " don't answer. Whoever it
is ! That's an order from me. Fall out the
officers ! " Four floppy-hatted, puttee'd subal-
terns walked briskly to him, aligned themselves
by the senior on the right, saluted, and walked
behind the skipper. " Company ! Dismiss."
Boots crunching on the loose muddy grey road :
loud slappings of right-hand fingers on rifle
stocks : a pause, and then the noise of two hundred men free for a time. At eight o'clock the

battalion marched away from the village of thatched, white-washed cottages. The rain had ceased. They marched towards an horizon of light, which was soundless except for the dull boom of a railway gun in front. The night was cool, with a mist straying in the flat of the wide valley they had entered. During the ten minutes of the second hour John Bullock leaned on the muzzle of his rifle, and watched the illuminated sky. He was thrilled by the silent running up and down, the noiseless expansion of flashes, the tremble and quiver of light. It was awful, and terrible, and lovely. Owing to the lie of the slow rising chalky downland, and the hollows of the valley, there was no sound of the cannon-ade ; only the ponderous and remote reverbera-tions of the railway gun ten miles in front of the battalion. Single flashes rose above the shimmering horizon, some flashing high and soundlessly ; then many flashed together, or so near together as to make a fluttering butterfly of light that was tremulant on the horizon before flitting into darkness, to rise again with luminous wings which multiplied and filled the whole sky marvellously with silent light. " Fall in ! Close up there ! By the right, quick march ! " They marched on towards the unknown, some in dread and foreboding, others imagining no further into time and space than the billets at the end of the march. At nearly three miles an hour the battalion marched along the tree-lined road, passing and being passed by lorries, motor-cars, motor-cycle dispatch riders, limbers, and waggons. The traffic was ceaseless. During one halt, while they were lying and standing on the right of the road, a criss-cross of searchlights began to move in the sky ahead of them, with the red pricks of anti-aircraft shrapnel. They

heard the far away bump of bombs. The order was passed down, " No smoking." They marched on, each man in a dark world of his own lighted with songs and comradeship, some brightly, others but dimly marching into the darkness without human horizon. The brighter sky-play

of soundless gun-fire gleamed in the water in the
ditches, it gleamed palely, very palely, on the
faces above the column of marching men ten
miles behind the line, still in country peaceful
and unbroken—though, by day, the rolling
cornlands were reburdened with dumps and
camps and horses and men everywhere. The
wings of light trembled and fluttered before
them, glimmering on the white walls of cottages
which they passed at midnight. The songs had
ceased, and the whistles ; they had ceased to be
living individual men who hoped. They marched
with their burdens because they must, on and on,
left-right, left-right, left-right, on heavy feet,
with aching shoulders. All thought of being
allowed to sleep on the ground as the ultimate
blessing. The moon rose out of the east, as something wasted and sick and forgotten above the
battlefields of the Somme. Each man slogged on
behind and beside other men, and when the order
came to halt, John Bullock sat down where he
stood and thought of nothing. His sweat became
chilly ; he stood on his hot and puffy feet, and
shook his arms. " Fall in ! We're nearly there.
Properly at ease everywhere ! " They had been
marching eight hours. John Bullock realized
some time later that the platoon in front was
leading off the road to the left. They had come to
the end of the night march, among dark wooden
huts with broken varnished-paper windows,
rickety doors, and deal plank floors roughened to
splinters by nailed boots. Here they chucked off

equipment, and not waiting for blankets from the transport, slept. Drubadrubadrubadrub— the huts shuddered in the gun-fire. In the morning it was seen to be a desolate bloody hole, like all the other camps John Bullock had been in. Some of the window frames and doors had been wrenched off for firewood by former battalions. No weeds grew under the wooden walls by the door, long since having been withered and rotted by the piss of tired soldiers coming there all the summer. The usual breakfast — black-brown congealed rasher of bacon, biscuits, a slice of dampish bread—someone said that the master-baker of Rouen, a staff sergeant-major, had been awarded the M.C.—plum-and-apple jam, and half-a-canteen of greasy tea. Rifles, gas-helmets, iron rations, ammunition, and field dressing inspection in the morning. No parade in the afternoon, but they were confined to camp. The Colonel and Adjutant and Company Officers rode away to look at the new sector they were taking over. There were rumours of attack. Some of the resting soldiers wrote home, others got down to it for a kip, a bit of shut-eye. Next day a talk on *Allied War Aims* by Captain Shanks. " I've got some bumff here I'm supposed to read to you," he said. " But you've heard all this balls before. We'll probably go over the top. I'm with you, boys ; remember, we're all together in this. If a shell's got my number on it, then that's that : if it hasn't, I shall be all right. Same with you. The odds are three to one on a blighty. That's all,

Sergeant-Major, dismiss the company." He was much liked by his men; and knew it. Battalion parade at 2 p.m. to go into the line. " We're for it, boys ! " cried the platoon sergeant. " They say Jerry's on 'is last ridge now : it's open country beyond ! " The platoon got ready for parade as though cheerfully. They marched under tall poplar trees, and came to a town of scarred red brick buildings and slate-scattered roofs. A flash, a yellow tinge in the air suddenly in front, a colossal crash. Grandmother, the railway gun, pooping off at Bapaume 20 miles away. They passed the gun on its multiple bogey carriage,

drawn backwards by its special engine. Albert
was crammed with lorries, waggons, ambulance
convoys, soldiers, mules, dumps of grey barbed
wire and shells by the railway sidings, hay,
sand-bags, and wooden trench-boards. German
prisoners were scraping the roads with shovels
and iron mud pushers. " How are yer, Jerry ?
Glad to be out of it ? " The Jerries nodded and
grinned with fellow-feeling ; a German under-
officer in charge of them, beside a kilted sentry
with slung rifle, did not smile, but saluted
Captain Shanks very rigidly, as he saluted every

officer that passed him. Under the tall red-brick cathedral ruin they marched. The chaps were looking up at the top of the tower. There it was : the Leaning Virgin. John Bullock recognized the gilt figure from photographs idly glanced at in the papers some weeks before. The war would be fini when it fell, the boys said. Some said it had been fastened by steel wire up there, at night, by Haig's secret order. " War over soon, what bloody 'opes ! " said a soldier, covered with mud from bristly chin to sandbagged legs, sitting by the wayside. " What's it like up there, mate ? Bad as Wipers ? " " Wipers ! Blime, old Wipers is cushy compared to this bleedun show ! " Roll on, Duration ! There were many halts on the long gradual straight road, bordered by stumps of trees, leading from the town. Before and behind them the two lines of up and down traffic were unbroken and continuous—guns and tractors, ambulance lorries, mules with flopping ears and hairy ribs and mud-rashed flanks. The wayside fields, seamed with wandering chalk heaps of old trenches and wire and pocked with shell-craters, were overgrown with fading long grasses. Upon the skyline thin dark bristles stood up ; these had been woods before July the First. More and more shell-holes ; a maze of foot-paths round the rims of shell-holes. A trench with rotting sand-bags on either side of the road : the murmur of voices repeating, " Our old front line ! " They stared, marvelling. Further on, the shell-holes were so thick and over-lapping that the whole

earth was tumbled brown and grey ; wire was
straggled about and buried in it. Wooden crosses
leaned everywhere in the old Noman's-land.
Blime, the boys must have copped a few packets
just about here ! A mass of stuff looking as
though it had been tipped out of a thousand
dust-carts lay to the right in the rusty broken
wire-belts and mess of trenches. An arrow sign-
board pointed, TO SITE OF LA BOISSELLE.
The mud was piled high beside the road, a
grey mud like mortar, in which John Bullock,
as he passed, saw embedded, rusty rifle barrels,

machine gun belts and twisted tripods, parts of waggons, tin hats, uniforms, haversacks, Lewis gun drum-buckets. On both sides of the road, which was aswim with liquid mud almost ankle deep above loose granite, gleaming grey-white with the sky, and pinkish where the shell-holes had been filled with bricks from the sites of villages, the waste land had been upheaved and blasted beyond living colour, shape, or movement, and then made soggy and finally drowned by the battlefield rains. Everywhere rifles bayonetted the ground, sometimes hung with

helmets. Drubberdrubberdrub continuous gun-
fire over and through all the living and the dead.
John Bullock saw men, single and in couples,
shuffling past them, answering no questions. Tin
hats on backs of heads, no tin hats, tin hats with
splinter-ragged sandbag-coverings ; men without
rifles, haggard, bloodshot-eyed, slouching past
in loose file, slouching on anywhere, anyhow,
staggering under rifles and equipment, some with
jaws sagging, puttees coiled mud-balled around
ankles, feet in shapeless mud boots swelled
beyond feeling, men slouching on beyond fatigue

and hope, on and on and on. G.S. waggons with loads of sleeping bodies. Stretcher-bearers plodding desperate-faced. Men slavering and rolling their bared-teeth heads, slobbering and blowing, blasting brightness behind their eye-balls, supported by listless cripples. Poor sods, thought John Bullock, and swallowed the spittle in his mouth. The halts were now more frequent ; the battalion was a khaki concertina, two deep to allow the downward traffic to pass. Duller grew the afternoon, brighter the flashes of the guns under the crest of the long, slow, bleak rise in front. They came to rubble heaps in the half light, and a board—SITE OF POZIERES. Already the sky beyond the high ground before them was hesitant with the wan white twilight pallor of the flares. Suddenly the dusk was split with light : instantly the air clapped stupendously in their ears. Curses of men were overborne by the uptearing and furrowing vast screech of a long-snouted naval gun in the ruins. The mules walked on, flop-eared and slow-stepping as before. Their hairy bellies and slack girths were clotted and hung with grey gobs of mud, as though swallows had started to build nests under them. The men marched over the ridge beyond the rubble heaps of the village site, and the air was rocked and buffeted by the gunfire which before had been like an oppressive and powerful drubberdrubberdrub against their heads. John Bullock saw the watery grey endless wastes of the battlefield glimmering and

gleaming with the flares which soared up in white
stalks and wavered as they drifted slowly down,
rising and wavering and falling from everlasting
to everlasting in the watery cold wastes of the
battlefield. Wheels rolled and jolted on. The
hot-bodied foot-sloggers followed. Many halts.
Curses. Brutal downward dronings of 5.9's.
Ruddy flashes in front. Cra-ash. Cra-ash. Cra-ash.
Cra-ash John Bullock breathed faster. Cries
came from far in front. Drivers crouched over
their mules. For Christ's sake get a move on in
front! They waited. The woo-r, woo-r, woo-r,

plop, woo-r plop, of gas-shells, the corkscrewing
downward sigh, the soft plop in the mud.
Another and another. Gas shells, ——— them.
From behind a voice crying, " Pass the word up
from the Second-in-Command to move on ! "
Other messages. Erz-z-z-z-z-ZAR, another salvo
over them like runaway tramcars, red-smoky
glares and spark-scatters and colossal rending
crashes. " The ——— are bracketing ; they'll
get us next," said the sergeant. Feet shuffling in
front and grate of wheels. They moved on. Other
shells glared and womped about the darkening
unknown around them ; and batteries flashed
away their shells in front, firing on enemy roads
and tracks. Before the crossroads they halted at
a dump. " 'Ere y'are ! Take this ! " John Bullock
had to carry a trench-board. At last they left the
long straight road and floundered off down a
track. Companies were now independent. A
Company advanced with 50 yards intervals between platoons. Darkness pressed upon each
man, darkness sucked at him from the mud,
often sucked oaths of blazing despair from his
muffled, floundering being. Past the zone of the
howitzers, whose immense orange-yellow flashes
seemed to hiss before the clang of light flung
hard squat shadows on the mud. The whole earth
seemed to flash each time a gun was fired ; the
tearing hiss of the shell grew remote in the soli-
tudes of the sky, and the flash seared itself with
dark intensity into their brains. They went on,
nearer the flares, breath harsh in mouths and

nostrils. " Sod all bully beef ! " grunted Ginger, and tipped the 48-lb. box on his shoulder into a shell-hole. Jesus Christ, how much farther ! The company, strung out, stopped at its head at intervals, to allow the stragglers to come up. Pass it up, not so fast in front. Pass it down, is No. 4 platoon closed up ? Lead on. Suck and slop of mud above ankles. Slither and flop and lurch and aching became unreal and everlasting. A hissing shriek, a flash, a clashing crack. Another. Another. Another. Whizz bangs. They were searching for 18-pounder battery positions, firing just in front of the company. It was now nearly

midnight, but John Bullock had no sense of time or space. He floundered in chaos, uncaring if he were hit ; but he flinched as the shells burst nearer. His mind seemed to work apart from his body, very small and far away, but quick and alert. They went on slowly past the field gun batteries. The long bright shafts of whitish light smacked the air, the shells screamed away just over their helmets. Each narrow light-blast was like concentrated moonlight. Surely the Germans would see them. His mind flung about in panic. Stop firing, for Christ's sake. Blinding light, paa-aa-ang of shell screaming away eastwards. The mud pulled at the top of his skull, hurting and wrenching it. How much farther ? Stiffies lying everywhere. Aoough, sickening stench. Chuck away the duck-board, heart slogging in ears, sick, red-blackness over eyes. John Bullock dropped the duck-board, and sat down, his chin resting on box-respirator. Couldn't go any further. After a rest he stood up, and having vainly tugged at the trench-board, drew his feet, clotted and heavy with suction at each slow step, along with the unspeaking others, as in a dream wherein terrible bright-bright-bright-brightness screeched itself into sudden smothering darkness. By one o'clock John Bullock and the dim-realized others were half-a-mile nearer the flares. Bullets fired from the German front lines tore the damp dark air around them, passing behind them. Flat reports of the rifles in front, the flat and mournful shearing of the bullets. Some whizzed, and made piping noises, crying in their downward spinning flight before the short *plap!* into the mud. The deep and dreadful night, the vast negation of darkness, in hopeless travail with the dead-weight of human and animal misery, was scored by the white streaks rising in a semi-circle before their lurching eyes. Burdened men, charred and splintered tree-stumps, overturned guns and limbers, leaning angle-iron pickets and thin scrawling wire tangles, were wavery with shadows homeless in the diffused pallor of everlasting flares. High explosive shells

falling in salvoes on the old German trench which the company was taking over. His life was dilated by every ruddy crash. The darkness pitched about. Somewhere an officer's voice cursing in high overwrought screams, mingling with the cries of men and the crack-crack-crack-crack of machine-gun fire, through the flares' greenish-powdery light. Sorry, sir, gasped John Bullock. Why the hell don't you look where you're going ? cried a voice. Silent, sodden figures shoved past him. Rain swished down before the relief was completed, glittering aslant with every white flash of the field guns. They were in the reserve line, with the battalion headquarters. Twenty minutes afterwards he was thinking that the dug-out was a bit of all right. Getting down had been a job. Blimey, what a stink at the wood-framed entrance, leading down so black and steep, very narrow. Wooden steps slippery with mud. Equipment and rifle caught and held and tripped him. Oh, hell. Anyhow, out of the mud. Below, narrow passages led left and right. His section went left, into a cube of space hardly undarkened by the flung-about little flame of a guttering candle. Tiers of bunks of wooden frames and rabbit-wire mattresses went up to the ceiling on three sides. Ceiling and walls and floor were lined with tongued-and-grooved pine boards. The air of the dug-out stank old and thick, sweaty, like a sour dish-cloth. " All Huns smell the same," said the sergeant ; "you're bloody lucky not to be in shell-holes to-night."

Sleep in equipment. Damn fine on the bunks :
to lie back hands under head and have a whiff at
a Red Huzzar ration fag. Bon for the troops.
They inhaled the sharp smoke, and sighed, content with nothingness in their minds. Later,
when the smoke of the officer's stove in the next
room made the eyes smart and breathing impossible, those in the top bunks began to grouse.
At last John Bullock got out and rolled himself in
the damp blanket. Christ, what an awful stink on
the floor. Rats scrambled and thumped inside
the boarding. One ran over the floor dragging its
scaly, pimply tail across his neck. Crrr ! You big,
lousy bastard ! Another. He climbed back into
the bunk : it was cold on the floor. He slept, and
was awakened by the corporal pulling his hand so
violently that he nearly fell off the wooden
frame. Come on, rouse up, where the hell d'you
think you are, in the ———— Ritz ? Up the sodding steps into the cold misty air of the flashing
sky, over the sodding parapet with screw pickets.
C.O. and Adjutant had got the bloody wind up,
afraid of being scuppered by a bombing raid, the
corporal said. Fixing screw-pickets out in front,
and untwisting and coiling the barbed wire
among them, while crack-crack-crack and pss
pss pss pss pss bullets went past in the flares'
unreal greenish light. Hourless hours of digging and clearing sump-holes in the trench and
fixing piles to rest the trench boards on. All back
half-an-hour before dawn, standing-to in the
trench, stamping feet in the squelch, blowing

through mitten'd hands. All wore woollen balaclava helmets over ears and under chins, tin-hat
chin strap shortened across back of head. Toeless
socks and puttee lengths taken off bolts ; right
upper pouches unclipped. Shells passed over in
the height of the sky, mostly from our guns. The
bluish ghastly chill light of dawn slowly morti-
fied the darkness. Jerry's machine-guns went
traversing just over the parapet, snipers' bullets
went thud into the bags, spluttering dirt about.
The C.S.M. came along with the rum. Jokes
began to be heard about the trench. Captain's
orders—No one to fire from the trench, or show
himself, or dig. The sun brought some cheer.
Breakfast was two biscuits and half a tin of bully.
No water. Ration party lost. Shells came over ;
they crouched and cringed for half-an-hour.
Phosgene gas lying about made cigarettes taste
like rotten eggs. No latrines. They squatted over
bully beef tins, and flung them, when used, over
the back of the trench. The day was weariness,
grey clouds and rain in the afternoon. They
waited for the darkness : unspeaking under
waterproof capes. Twilight and the first flares
and the sudden screaming gust of traversing
machine guns. The wind rushed in the darkness,
flinging the rain in squalls. John Bullock was in
the ration fatigue party of an officer, a sergeant
and thirty other men. He was glad to be moving.
He was wet and cold from neck to knees; no feeling
in feet. Soon he was warm. All the night was
before them for the job. Every brilliant white

blast from the field-guns blanched and froze the gleaming and linked watery shell-holes. Every blast must surely show them up for miles. Paa-aang, Paa-aang. Paa-aang. Paa-ang. Paa--ang. Paa-ang. The shocks of whitest light staggered him, rotted with mud after every sucking step. The officer fell into a shell-hole. The battery fired thirty shells while they were trying to pull him out, and two others who sunk as he rose up. They crawled out, big and ragged with stinking mud, beyond swearing. John Bullock tried to scrape the mud off the officer with the rim of his tin hat.

They glided on afterwards, their boots almost
pulled off at every step, although they were trying to walk in boot-holes already made. Paa-
aang—wiffwiffwiffwiff of shell rising eastwards in
the utterly black after-blast. He began to enjoy
the light-blasting feeling. He imagined a girl
smiling in the darkness : the secret stealing away
to some quiet deserted dug-out. He allowed
others to pass him, to be alone with the light-
blasts giving him the soft glances for his desire.
Slurring downward corkscrews of sound, flooerflooerflooer-plop, flooerflooerflooer-plop flooer-

flooerflooer-plop, flooer-pop, flooer-pop, flooer-pop. The white luring of the celestial-satanic female merging into his body fled away in the fear of green-cross gas shells, searching for the 18-pounder batteries. He adjusted his box-respirator, and floundered on, his face and sight sweating and misty. The rain squalls lashed him. He tore off his mask. He and his chum Ginger had the job of carrying back a canteen of hot soup, fixed to the poles of a stretcher. When they arrived back at battalion headquarters the soup was a-slop with cracked cakes of grease, but it was warm. During the hour-and-a-half journey from the transport cookers John Bullock had been thinking of a drink of soup when they got back ; but as soon as they arrived the sergeant-major ordered them to follow " A " Company ration party to the front line. The quarter-mile journey took more than an hour, for the communication trenches were knee-deep in water and sludge. The soup tasted of bacon fat and coal-smoke ; but it was wet. Many stiffies were lying out in front, both Jocks and Jerries. Some of the boys went scrounging. No good, though, for every haversack had been pulled open, every pocket had been slit up, and every finger-ring cut off. The front line had been heavily shelled by their own guns that morning, and seven men had been knocked out, two killed. Bleedun fine staff work, I don't think. Five of the seven had got back to the aid post : lucky sods, they were out of it. Any rumours about the Kayser asking for

peace ? What about the Russian steamroller ?
————— the Russian steamroller. You couldn't,
old son, for the ————— silly thing was always
going the wrong way. The next night John
Bullock's company went up to the front line,
walking over the top beside the flooded communication trench. Jerry was two hundred
yards away, but very quiet, except for fixed
rifles firing by dug-out doors and down communication trenches. And snipers. Drubadruba-
drub went the guns down south. Playing up hell
down there, where the Froggies were next to the

English. The sky bubbled with clouded light. The old German trench where John Bullock's company stood was in fairly good condition. The sides were revetted with timber and expanded metal. It glitter-quaked in the flashes with mud and water to the knees. They walked and stood about in the long grass between the craters behind. Time was suspended, the night endlessly unreal. Only the thought of others being there the same as he was made John Bullock not think of what was happening. One poor sod had tied the end of his pull-through cord to the trigger of his rifle and then to his boot, and put the muzzle

against the roof of his mouth, and blown the top of his head off. He'd been out two years, they said. If you didn't kill yourself properly they got you well in hospital and then court-martialled you, and you were shot tied to a post. S.I.W.—Self-Inflicted Wounds. People at home never knew how you were done for when you were in France. Endlessly unreal the night. Fingers so numb that they could not find buttons or brace tags. To bend legs was to feel them grown into a tree trunk, vast without feeling. While John Bullock was painfully fumbling at the sodden leather of the brace-tags he saw a low, weak flash over Jerry's lines, and heard a small,

dull report. Sentry crying *Minnie up!* John
Bullock saw a red spark in the sky over
Noman's-land. It seemed to come down very
slowly. Splap! it hit the mud on the right about
forty yards away. He could see the sparks. It
fizzed like a cracker. GET DOWN. He flung himself flat. RED ROA-AAR. Afterwards he slid
down into the trench. His trousers were sagging,
and he tried to fasten the buttons with mud-
clotted hands. *Minnie up left!* Another red spark
wiggling overhead. GET DOWN. Splap! Pause.
RED RAAAAR. Every minute for twenty
minutes the oil-drums hummed over. The officer

ordered them to lie down twenty yards behind
the trench in shell-holes. Rain lashed down again.
The minnies stopped. Flashes behind, shells
screaming over just above their heads, and
bursting along the German front line. One gun
kept firing short, the shells falling in their own
line. Heavy stuff began to go over. Stuff to give
the bastards. Soon above the German trenches
the white shrapnel smoke was almost continuous
in the quick-rising flares. A red line streaking up,
a cluster of green stars falling away ; another
rocket going up, and white stars ; a third broke

green. Now we're for it, thought John Bullock, pushing his legs down in the water of the shell-hole, and tilting his helmet over the side of his head as he pressed his ear into the space of his elbow crook. The awful downward buzzing of German shells began to come, falling behind along the support line. CRASH CRASH CRASH CRASH, each enormously awful, making him all thin and hollow, only a heart knocking in a painful throat. He felt himself becoming liquid and dead in the mud. This feeling went from him when he saw he was between the two barrages. Flares were swishing up many at a time. The officer came slipping along, crying, *Stand to ! Stand to ! They may be going to raid !* The hollow feeling came back as he thought of bayonets, of the scream he would give as the long, thin steel broke into his belly. Ah well, I don't give a sod what happens. I'll keep a shot until the very last and shoot as he points. He pulled the sock from the bolt, and slipped it over the butt, pushing it under his right shoulder strap. The bolt worked hard with mud. Flip, one cartridge wasted. He pushed it home, and waited. Two red rockets rose together from battalion headquarters behind. Our S.O.S. The sky behind became a jagged sheet of continuous flashing : the shells roared over and crashed like the furnace of a gigantic train reflected on its smoke. The sergeant came along, shouting something, and waving his rifle. He looked pissed, as though he'd been half-inching the rum. Don't fire until the

officer fires the Verey light signal, he bawled. A
machine gun began firing on the right. Rifle fire
crackled along the front. A mort-blast of bullets
began to sweep over the German lines. He heard
shouting, and saw the red spurts of rifles. He
began firing, as fast as he could, trembling and
cursing as he knelt up to pull another clip from
his pouch. He fired until his bolt jammed, and
then lay still, waiting. What did it all mean ?
The Boche raid had failed ; there were cries out
in front, and our Lewis guns firing bursts to cop
the rescuers. Some time later John Bullock was
trying to fill sandbags with mud, heaving them
up on the parapet, squelching shapeless bags
oozing and dripping, falling down and splashing.
O CHRIST ALMIGHTY his mind flared and
shrieked, after the hours of dredging with aching
back and arms and neck and banging level with
hardly-able-to-be-lifted shovel. The gangrenous
light of dawn began to spread over the German
lines ; they dragged themselves away to the
stand-to. The rations, including the rum, had
gone in the bombardment. They stood about in
the trench, thinking of nothing, half asleep, leaning up against the parapet, or trying to wash
their rifles in the water. John Bullock saw the
High Street, the hawkers' barrows, the shops,
the picture palace lights, the tramcars—there
was a clang like a tramcar bell, a splash, and
Ginger, who had been looking out over Noman's-
land, slid down into the water. John Bullock and
the corporal pulled his head out, and held him

up. Blood ran down from a hole in his right temple. The back of his head was open like an egg, hairy with thick blood and broken-sploshed grey brains. He snored and gurgled and twitched. Blood trickled from his ears and mouth; he kicked, blew blood bubbles from his nostrils. They heaved him up over the parados when dead. That night the stretchers took the body back with nine others, to battalion headquarters, where a fatigue party, including John Bullock, buried them all in a 5.9 shell-hole after a short burial service by " Cheero Boys," the padre.

Cheero Boys went up the line to speak to the boys, after managing to scrounge a double whack of soup for the burial party. The following night they went back into rest billets—on the road where more loose granite had been tipped. They walked as though broken glass were in their boots, to a waste ground of shell-holes near Pozieres, the only shelter being ground-sheets laced together over bits of wood found in the ruin which had been picked over by tens of thousands of scrounging hands. The 60-pounder battery, firing in the ruins, put out their bivvy

candle-flames with every white overhead blast.
They slept soundly. It rained, and rained, and
rained. The division remained on the Somme
until the great frosts of the New Year ; and when
the soldiers began to dread the effect of shells
bursting on contact with the icy ground, the
German artillery suddenly pulled out, and went
north, some said to Arras, where a Big Push was
being planned. The cry was no longer Roll on,
Duration. The first seven years will be the worst,
they said to each other, avoiding, in the sem-
blance of jest, the reality on which their minds
refused to dwell.

FOURTH PHASE

IN the rainy autumn of 1917 John Bullock remembered the cushy days on the Somme with regret. He was dreading the imminent attack which the battalion was practising on dummy trenches, in gas-masks, amidst smoke. The battalion was supposed to be resting : arms drill, bayonet fighting, box-respirator drill, physical jerks, saluting drill, bombing parades, etc., etc. And every other afternoon fatigue parties left in lorries which dumped them in Ypres, through

whose crumped heaps of grass-grown bricks and
mortar they marched to the forward dumps along
roads swilling with mud and bordered with
jagged tree-stumps and broken limbers. Very
soon the road disappeared with the tree-stumps.
Baulks of teak and beech, tipping and splashing

under their feet, continued the road. Rifles, dead
horses and mules with liquid pinkish matter running out of the gashes in their skins, waggons,
stretchers, telephone wire, shells and bombs and
shreds of water-proof capes and helmets, were
piled high beside the track. There were no

trenches and no shell-holes ; all had been shifted and re-shifted by the shell-blasts, until all were decayed and roughly levelled in the water which gleamed with the sunless sky. On the Somme most of the dead had been buried ; here they were spreading into the ground where they had fallen, each with several holes around its cloth-rotten spreading place, where the rats had tunnelled. Many tanks lay on flat and brown misty water-waste, half and three-quarter sunken away. Tanks rent and shattered, the bodies of their crews swelled, with green faces, old gashes and breaks dripping black. Duckboard paths led out from the infirm and wandering baulk tracks, which were under fire all day and all night, because they were heaving somewhere with feet and hoofs and wheels all day and all night. At night they were thick as ribbed serpents' corpses in the slime, congested with wheeled and footed maggots. Long strings of mules and horses, each led by a driver, with shells in wicker panniers. Carrying and working parties. Troops going in and coming out. Stretcher-bearers of German deserters and prisoners carrying wounded. John Bullock took no heed of the dead men, nor of the wounded on the stretchers. He was just kept going by one hope : the hope of getting a wound which would put him out of the war. After nine weeks on the Somme his feet had swollen and gone red, and he had got down to the base with them. The court of enquiry had held him blameless, for he had

been clever enough to tell the truth, and the
infantry officers on light duty at the base com-
prising the court would not have got a man a
Field General Court Martial if they could wangle
out of it. He had lost the little toes of each foot,
but this had not been enough to get him a B or a
C category. He had returned to another battalion of his regiment in a draft of three hundred
and ninety-two other men, just after an attack
on the Hindenburg Line on the left of Bullecourt
in May, 1917, when the survivors before the uncut wire had crawled back at night, leaving six
hundred dead and wounded out of the seven
hundred who had gone up the night before. The
next big show had been against Whitesheet Hill
on 6th June, when the mines had gone up, and
Messines been taken. Only two hundred casualties ; most of them gassed when going in on Y/Z
night. John Bullock had remained behind with
thirty other men of the company and an officer,
as a reserve. He was terrified of the idea of going
over the top. Every time the brutal droning of
shells increased into the deep, savage, sudden
buzzing which told they were going to burst
near, he crouched and sweated and cringed. He
had spent a month at Etaples with trench fever,
which some said was caused by the bite of lice :
these chaps said they hadn't loused themselves,
hoping to get the fever. His half-sleeping was
sharp and jagged with fearful dreams ; he
chewed cordite, as recommended by an old
sweat swinging the lead in the ward, got from a

cartridge when the bullet had been worked out.
It gave him a headache, but would it increase
his temperature ? Fear of being rumbled had
made him chuck his little store into the latrine.
Then had come the mutiny at the Old Tipperary
Camp, the boys being fed-up with all the bloody
slaughter going on up in the salient, battalions
going in seven hundred strong and coming out
seventy after a few hours, and being made up to
strength and going in again, and nothing doing
except a fresh layer of stiffs and wounded on top
of the others. The mutiny had begun with the
organized defiance of orders at the Bull Ring ;
the streaming back of thousands of men singing
and cheering ; the shooting of the sergeant of
the Gordon Highlanders by an N.C.O. of the
Military Field Police, a bloody great hulking
swine of an ex-champion heavy-weight boxer
dodging the column at the base, who used to
twist the arms and legs of the insubordinate
Australian soldiers doing Field Punishment No.
I. He ran like hell, and hid in the R.T.O.'s office.
John Bullock had seen the A.P.M., who was said
to have been a North West Mounted Policeman
in Canada before the War, rolled in the road. The
General had tried to address them—" Are you
Englishmen, or are you blackguards ? "—and
had been told to put a sock in it. " See here,
general, you've been doing all the talking so far,
and now it's the turn of the Poor Bloody Private
Soldier." Then the hunt of the red-caps through
Etapps ; the looting of the estaminets ; the Aus-

tralians sent down from the line to stop the mutiny of more than 100,000 men ; the Aussies joining in. " War's over, Jerry's fed up, so are we. Jerry didn't want the war, nor did we. It's only the bloody profiteers who want it to go on. They are the enemies of the masses." Some said that junior officers had been disguised as private soldiers in order to get into the estaminets and spot the organizers of the mutiny ; after them had come the break-up patrols armed with entrenching tool handles, laying out the leaders when found. A posh battalion of territorials from G.H.Q.; machine guns on the bridge over the river ; no food ; the end of the wild hopes of going home and seeing wives and kids and mothers and girls again. Dozens of poor sods handcuffed wrist to wrist, two by two, outside the Commandant's office, awaiting court martial and the firing squad. That was the end of that ! And the War went on as usual, and the Bloody Butcher sending in the division again and again and getting them ———d up to hell. Thus our hero's thoughts as he carried what, many times during the many times he rested beside it on the duckboard track, he swore at as a sodding great lump of firewood. The bloke following him was fed-up too : he shouted out as he let his load slide off his shoulders, " Let the bleedun brass hats come and carry their —— matchsticks ! " They both crouched up as shrapnel clanged over a solitary snapped tree in the morass. John Bullock's dumb mental agony sweated itself away.

He lumbered on, reached the dump, and hurried back after the others to the dump beyond Bridge No. 4. Wipers, with the sun on it, looked like the long white jaw-bone of a mule, with its teeth chipped and splintered, its jaw-bone cracked and shot away. It was dark when the exhausted

fatigue party reached the camp in the area of oak woods near Poperinghe. The curved elephant iron roof sides of the Nissen huts built close together were rusting through the faded camouflage paint-splotches. Forty men and a sergeant

slept in each hut. Sand-bags covered the windows beside the door, shutting in the draughty candle-gleams. Muffled bangs in the distance ; wop, wop, wop, the soft noises of archie shells high up in the sky. Oh Gawd, more bloody eggs ! The bombing raids were made every night on the camps. Those not asleep lay still and listened for the throbbing hum of the big bombing planes. One man, an elderly Scotsman named Wishart, a stretcher-bearer, solemnly sat up on his bed of boards and put on his tin-hat, and knelt up and prayed his usual silent prayer. Then he lay down with hat tilted over his nose, ignoring the usual jokes. He was the father of seven children. They called him Daddy Washout. He was forty-six years old, very earnest, very anxious to do everything properly, and made a jerky mess of everything, fixing his bayonet, piling arms, rolling his puttees, etc. They're coming over ! cried a young soldier excitedly, not long out from home. " Oh, go and shit," called out a man who had been a young soldier a year before. Put a sock in it ! said the sergeant, and they listened to the spinning hiss of a falling bomb. It womped into the

next camp, they judged. " If 'tis the Lord's will, we'll be struck, not else, boys," said Daddy Washout. Replies of Heem numbah Nanety nane, Amen. There will be no collection. You can't put the ——— wind up us, mate, etc., interrupted by a loud swishing noise swelling into a whining shriek, the figures of soldiers in pants and shirts leaping out of bed. FLASH. They were all mixed up together and crying out. Flash—flash —WOMP—WOMP—other cries from the middle of the camp. Three in the hut were killed. They had to scrape one off the curved iron hut wall with an entrenching tool. They stood round in silence in the acrid chilly night air, watching the small weak spots of an electric torch light, while the bits were taken away on stretchers. One wounded chap with his arms blown off, the stumps charred with permanganate of potash, chucked on in handfuls by the R.A.M.C. orderlies to make the stumps like leather. It was different from seeing a chap cop it up the line. John Bullock's mind was relaxed when out at rest ; death entered with thoughts that it might have been him. The mind closed again, turned away from FEAR. Bombs and more bombs, two and three raids a night. The place was lousy with troops. They toiled at sandbag filling, laying them header-and-stretcher deep four feet up the sides of the huts. The Brigade working and carrying parties up the line took between ten and fourteen hours from leaving to returning. The only thing they lived for now was (1) a Blighty

one ; (2) the hours spent in the estaminets ; (3) sometimes a bit of dick. And one morning as he was filling sandbags, listening to Nobby Clark telling about a red-lamp house, John Bullock thought he would do it too, before he was bloody well snuffed out. He had often heard the boys talking about having a bit of dick in the red lamps, and had been slightly repelled and disgusted with the idea. Terrible to go with anyone like that. He had seen queues of the chaps waiting outside, as though it were for the pit or gallery of a theatre ; the M.P.'s keeping near

to see they didn't start rough-housing. John Bullock used to think that he would never lower himself to go with anyone he didn't really love. Now with an inner thrill of exultation he said to himself that he didn't care what happened. His fears left him as he decided to see what it was like—the haunting fears of himself lying half in a shell-hole with neck and hands and body swelled dirty greeny-grey and face like an old loaf sodden in mud. What was the song old Crimp, the post

corporal, used to sing, old Crimp who'd been out
since Mons :

> *We don't give a damn for Will-i-am,*
> *We know the Crown Prince is barmy ;*
> *We don't give a —— for old Von Kluck*
> *And all his bleeding old army !*

Stuff to give 'em. He would go to Pop the next
day, and he'd paint the place red. John Bullock
imagined that he had been drunk many times
before ; he thought himself, privately, to be a lad
when he had three-quarters of a bottle of vin
rouge inside him, with a couple of beers, a
cognac, a few café rhums, mixed up with greasy

chips fried in horse and mule fat, telling everyone how bloody tight he was, and laughing and
singing, or rather shouting until the inevitable
spewing after closing time. Eat, drink, and be
merry—all on a bob a day—for to-morrow—to-
morrow he'd paint the town red. Nobby Clark
said he'd go with him and show him the ropes.
Nobby said he knew a nice little place just off the
Grand Place, where there were some proper little
pushers. Pretty, grinned John Bullock. Artists at
the game, Nosey my boy, Nobby assured him.
That evening in the Divisional Follies he watched

one of the men dressed up as a girl in the show, and thought of the morrow. She would have shy, soft eyes veiled in long lashes : she would fall in love with him : he would make a night of it ! He was a lad ! If only the chaps in the office could see John Bullock, Esquire, with Nobby Clark, Esquire, on the way to visit a lady ! Return to hitting a typewriter, after the War ? I don't think, papa ! In, out, on guard ! They said the phosphorous shells isolated the pill-boxes so that the machine gunners couldn't see to fire, dense white smoke choking them through the splayed slits. One to three, the chance of death if you were hit. Well, some good boys had gone where he might go ! Who cared a damn what happened? Not John Bullock. They walked out of the camp singing cheerily

> *I want to go home,*
> *I want to go home,*
> *I don't want to go to the trenches no more,*
> *Where the guns and whizz-bangs and*
>   *cannons do roar,*
> *I want to go home,*
> *Where the Alleman can't get at me,*
> *O my, I don't want to die,*
> *I want to go home.*

They ate eggs and chips in a wayside hut made of bits of wood and iron assembled at odd times by a peasant whose home used to be in Gheluvelt. Nosey and Nobby shared a bottle of plinketty plonk, as *vin blanc* was called. The wife was old and bulky with soiled black clothes. Bully bif no

bon, non, she said, shaking her head. She had a
store of blue tins, enough to last her life out, and
the life of her husband : she said bully bif no bon
to all soldiers before serving, meaning they must
pay 1 fc. 50 each in cash. A little child came into
the hut, and she drove it out with what she
called a *martinet*, a short-handled, short-lashed
whip, a photograph of which John Bullock had
recently seen in an English newspaper, as having
been found in captured German trenches, evidence of the brutal Hun officer. Anyhow, all the

papers are liars, said Nobby to Nosey. Afterwards they had a few drinks in a buvette, and
set out for the knocking shop. Outside the
estaminet in the rue d'Hôpital John Bullock was
overcome with apprehension ; and, saying that

he had the squitters, and would come back, he
left Nobby and walked rapidly away. Alone, he
had some more drinks in The Parrot, a boozer
called after the grey and red patriotic bird in the
room, who could swear in English, and who,
when a glass was held near his beak, with the

words " Here's to the Kayser," replied in its
glass-cutting voice, " ——— the Kayser." Feeling the life surge in him, John Bullock said to
himself : You're getting tight, you know, Nosey,
my boy. He went out into the street to look for

a bit of skirt. He saw one across the square, and
whacked his swagger cane, which he had just
bought for a franc, against his puttee'd leg.
Whistled. A motor car with a pennant on its
bonnet passed him, with three brass hats in it,
one of them an old toff with a round head and a

great white moustache, whom he recognised as
the Butcher. John Bullock sprang to attention,
and gave the Guardee waggle behind the right
ear ; the Butcher barely acknowledged it with a
wave of his finger as the car rushed past, driven
by a superior private soldier in a hat, almost an
officer's hat, and a tunic almost an officer's tunic.
Well, well, some gets the fat, and some gets the
lean, as the bloke in the Follies used to recite in
Mending the 'ole in the Road. John Bullock un-
stiffened, and crossed the road. He went back to
the knocking shop, and after a brief hesitation

before the double doors, entered by a side door. Chaps playing crown-and-anchor in a corner. Others sitting at tables, hats on backs of heads, smoking and laughing, glasses before them. They ignored his entry. An interior door opened and a broad, almost harsh, woman's voice shouted out a word that he couldn't catch. A man jumped up, grabbed his hat, and went out of the door, leaving them grinning at each other. Then the pontoon players picked up more cards, and the group round the crown-and-anchor board went on placing their money on the crown-and-anchor board. This was a worn folding square of cloth marked with six sections, corresponding to Heart, Crown, Diamond, Spade, Anchor and Club ; called, heart, Major (sergeant-major), Dinkie, Curse, Mud-hook and Shamrock. " Lay your money single and pick up double. You lay and we pay, the good old Sweaty Sox, out since Mons, often bent but never broke, the rough and tough, the old and bold. If you don't speculate you can't accumulate. Come along, gentlemen, you are not on parade. Who fancies the lucky old Major ? Copper, silver and gold. You come in rags and ride away in motor-cars. Back your judgment, gentlemen. The Mud-hook, the Curse, the Heart, the Major. Now then, up she comes !" A pile of torn and dirty paper notes and silver lay within the crook of the banker's left arm on the table. As it grew it was crammed into his pockets. He was an A.S.C. driver, rumoured to be worth a hundred thousand francs. One after

another a man got up from a chair or left the
crowd around the board, pinched out his fag and
stuck it behind his ear, and went out of the door
after the deep " Next " of madame. She served
the drinks, grumbling at the tattered, dirty
notes offered her. The only dirt she recognised
was on paper money. John Bullock was the
eighteenth. He had entered the place at 16 hours;
his turn came just before 17 hours 30 minutes.
That old woman led him upstairs. She wore a
leather pouch like a tram driver. It jingled with
money. Beyond the open door he saw a fattish

half-undressed woman. He could not look at her, after the first glance. She had thick ankles and legs in coarse black stockings. The room smelt musty. He wished he hadn't come. " Fife ! " said Madame in her fat double-chinned voice. " Fife," holding up five fingers. He gave her a note. " Champagne," he said recklessly, and gave her three five-franc notes. She smiled, "Now spik to Susanne. She spik English. Quite clean girl. She make you much happiness." Suzanne dangled a hand towards him. He went forward. The door was shut. She looked up and smiled. He tried to overcome his reluctance, increased by the sight of spittle on the floor. " Don't be shy, old soldier," she said. " Non," he said, and waited. " Poor, bloody Tommee," she smiled sidelong at him. " This bloody war no bloody good, eh ? " He began to feel better and dared to stroke her head. She caught his hand and put one of his fingers in her mouth, then pulled him down on the couch beside her, and began to mess him about. Then the booze came. He swallowed a couple of glasses, and convinced himself, supporting her heavy bulk on his knees, that he was beginning to feel as he should have felt. He grew rough as he overcame his unmanly shame, and she swiped him across the ear, and cursed him in a hard, deadly voice, mixing English and Flemish words and phrases, from which he flinched as from a machine gun burst in Noman's-Land at night. She told him to —— off out of here, the ——— smeerlop, the dirty Ingleesh stoomerkloit, etc. Then, seeing his eyes, she twined her arms round his neck and fastened her mouth hard against his mouth and pulled him down on the couch. His mind and senses could not fuse into oneness and abandon. Trying to ward off his

reluctance he strove to feel as he imagined he ought to feel, lest she become impatient and despise him as an ungrown-up weakling. Only when, in desperation at the raps of the old woman on the door, he thought himself into the physical likeness of Nobby Clark, did he get rid of himself

and achieve some sort of freedom. Afterwards he
put on his coat and belt and cap and went out
without a word, unable to look at her. He slipped
out of the estaminet, a part of England that has
sought, in vain, to find its inner sun. He went
back to the estaminet where he had had a few
drinks before. Drubadrubadrubadrub. More
slaughter up there in the mud. Poor sods. His
turn soon. What did anything matter ? You had
to die sometime. Old Ginger was gone, and all
his old pals. Well, what odds if he went where
Ginger was, and all the boys. He had some more

wine in The Parrot and thought of the old days before the UTTERLY GONE FOR EVER. His mind refused. He gulped more wine. Why was it happening, everyone wanted it to stop, the Frogs and the Jerries, and all the boys, so why did it go on ? There was no God, or He wouldn't have . . . Pretending to be asleep, he hid his head in his arms to hide his tears, and fell asleep, from which he awakened with a mouth feeling like the bottom of the parrot's cage in the corner of the room. Madame, ong otre bottle de vang rooshe ! Merci, m'sieu. He stayed there until

chucking out time at nine pip emma, all his money gone, one of a little band of drunks and semi-drunks who thought it was the finest evening of their lives, and sang *Jolly Old Pals*, and *Wipe the Tear Baby Dear from your Eye-ee* until the inhuman Military Police, revolver holster'd and red-capped, came in, and they scattered. He reached camp after the early morning parade having shot his bundle—Salient slang for vomiting an excess of drink—in several instalments on the way to International Corner. He was very unsteady on his legs, and the regimental

police took him into the guard tent. In spite of
his protests his puttees and boots and belt were
taken off and his hands were tied behind him to
the base of the tent pole. An official act of kind-
ness ; a drunken man might fight, and so aggra-
vate his crime. Next morning he went before his
company officer, and was remanded for the
Commanding Officer's orderly room. Outside the
C.O.'s room the stones were spotlessly white-
washed. At last his turn came. Sergeant-Major
shouting : Cap off ! Another official benevolence :
lest it be thrown at the C.O. in anger, a court-

martial offence. Accused and escort, Tsh'n!
Right turn! Quick march! Right wheel! Left
wheel! 'Alt! Right turn! Terrific heel click and
salute. 19023, Private J. Bullock charged with
first, Being drunk on Active Service; second,

Being absent off parade. The evidence was given.
What had he to say? Very sorry, sir. Won't do
it again, sir. A very serious crime, to be drunk
on active service, and missing a parade. Sup-
posing the battalion had gone up into the line?
John Bullock stood very still before the C.O.,

sick and head-aching, brooding subconsciously
on the chance of a dose. He tried to forecast from
the words what sort of punishment he would get.
The Adjutant placed the rustling crime-sheet
before the C.O. The soldier looked at the officer,
at his clean tunic and row of ribbons, at his
highly-polished brown boots and spurs under the
blanket-covered trestle table ; he felt that life
was dark and hopeless. During the instant that
the Colonel glanced at the crime-sheet he saw the
War as something he had never truly thought of
before : something that kept millions of men

like himself in slavery. If you dared to say it was slavery and ought to be stopped, you would get handcuffed like those chaps down at Etaples. " Fourteen days' field punishment No. 1," said the C.O. Prisoner and escort, right turn ! Quick march ! Right wheel ! Halt ! Left turn ! Cap on ! Right turn ! Quick march ! To the guard tent. Thenceforward John Bullock went with every carrying and working party up the line ; but when the others were sleeping exhaustedly, he was doing pack drill on the square ; emptying the latrine buckets, shifting a heap of heavy stones from one part of the parade ground to

another, and then back again to the same place, and back again to the other place, walking on a path of his own mud ; afterwards he was tied to the guard-tent pole with his arms above his head. The armed sentry who accompanied him every-where, even to the latrine, changed every twenty-four hours, but every one, after a period of silence, spoke to him like a pal. One gave him a fag. John Bullock wished he hadn't. At last he had realized the War. He wouldn't come back from the attack. Roll on, the attack ! The bat-talion paraded for an inspection by many generals, led by the short, stocky figure nicknamed,

humorously, The Butcher. Again they marched
out to the dummy trenches, and with horsemen
to represent the creeping barrage, and cyclists to
represent tanks, they made the attack ; walking
forward in gas masks at the rate of a hundred
yards every three minutes. They perfectly
stormed a pill-box, surrounding it with rifle
grenades of one section, while the Lewis gunners
gave covering fire from the flank to the bayonet
men and the phosphorous bombers. The afternoon before going up to the attack was spent in
lying easy, writing letters home, and sleeping.
John Bullock was still under armed-guard. At
five o'clock he paraded in battle order with his
company. They drew two bombs each, and three
bandoliers of rifle ammunition. Each man's
helmet was already covered with sandbag-cloth.
The divisional colours were already painted on
the side, and sewn on the arms of their tunics
just under the brass shoulder-strap numerals.
The company officers were dressed exactly like
the men, and they carried rifles. The regimental
chaplain regarded them with a cheerful smile
hiding his sadness as they marched away to the
long convoy of grey motor-buses drawn up along
the Poperinghe road. He was going later with the
medical officer to the battalion aid post, whence
he would wander off to seek the wounded lying
out, to comfort them, if he could, with his words.
He was one of those rare men who carried the
real War on their shoulders. He knew he could
not say what he thought, so he did all he could to

help the men, whom he understood, with his personal sympathy. And he went where they went. After the War it will be different, he used to think : out of this great agony will survive a new spirit . . . The soldiers liked him, and called him " Cheero Boys." One behind the other, the grey —once London red—motor buses, their windows boarded up, took the battalion through the pavé of Poperinghe, swinging to the left through the long, straight street of houses, and through the avenue of trees whose leaves a wild evening wind was strewing over the sodden fields. On through

Brandhoek with its light-chinks in the crocked cottages, through Vlamertinghe, with the holes in its tumbling church-tower, and messed-up brick-and-rafter heaps on either side. The bigger guns were flashing and banging, but it was quiet up in the Salient, where the white flares were endlessly rising up and floating down. John Bullock crouched, rifle between knees, on the top of a bus, trying to prevent himself thinking about not being himself that time to-morrow. The other soldiers were quiet, too, each one withdrawn into himself. They were passing Goldfish Chateau, where a lot of white-and-blue-banded dispatch riders were standing about. Over the railway lines and along the last bit of straight into Wipers. A double flash, the succeeding womp, womp. Nobby Clark made a joke out of his nervousness ; they all felt very exposed on the top of the bus. Over lock N. 10—didn't they all know that stinking hole—and on, up past the high dark ruins of the prison, round the corner of the empty shell-holed prison yard, and the Cook's Tour was over. " Oh, oh, oh, it's a lovely war," sang Nobby. " Come on, boys ; it's going to be a walk-over ! " John Bullock felt easier, he liked Mr. Maddison, his platoon officer, always a cheery word for them, a proper toff. He felt better still as soon as they were marching along through the ruins lit up by the flash of howitzers. Once, when they stopped, he saw candlelight flung about in a cellar below the road level. The gas-blanket was swaying in the wind.

He had a glimpse of a tablecloth, plates, a loaf,
a whiskey bottle and mug, a magazine ; wildly
he imagined himself sitting there in paradise.
Perhaps never see home any more, mother's face,
hearing his death. O why, why was the War ?
Death was darkness, good-bye for ever. FOR-
EVER. He couldn't go over the top. No, no.
Over the top was terrible. DEATH. He couldn't.
Mum and Dad waving from 94, Burntash Road,
mother saying prayers, sweet gentle face, O God
the Father, God the Son, God the Holy Ghost,
do not let me die, let him see mother again, and

Dad, O God I've been wicked, I won't do it again, God. Brutal downward droning, the coarse, fat, buzzing roar of shells, down, DOWN. Three ruddy glares linked in one, seen bright through shut eyes and clenched teeth ; the light blasted through him. Whizz, Wang, Zip. Crack. Jagged splinters. " Come on, old soldiers, get a move on, lead on there ! " cried Mr. Maddison. The scattering, loose file moved together again and led on, through the low heaps of grass-grown bricks and over the cross-roads to the St. Julien road. The wind blew in gusts over the dark

morass, puckering the watery wastes like a toad's back. The extra weights—bombs, 150 extra rounds, shovel in haversack on shoulders, extra iron ration—began to ache the shoulders. They swung left and had the flares before them. Shells passed overhead, scoring the sky, and burst with a heavy, thunderous womp behind them in Ypres. Their paces became closer. They stood in the rain. Shuffled on. Stood about. Shuffled on. Wet and shivering. Stamped their squelching boots. They scarcely heeded the faint cries coming out of the roadside transport wreckage. Rain lashed across the black nihilism of the old battle wastes, the wind wailed through the wreckage of tilted and sky-gaping tanks, the wind slashed the corners of their ground-sheet capes across their cheeks, wrinkling the water, and blew some sitting into the mud. He could see the man in front of him as a hump of slow black. Soon the ruined roadway ended in the morass. The timber baulks quaked and splashed and sank away under the tread. He fell over old and new bodies of mules and men. He clawed himself round the almost continuous scatter of limbers and mules and gurgling wounded, all rough-cast with greyish mud. A shadow moved by one limber, lurching out from the wheel over which it had been sagging, a shadow mowing and gibbering at John Bullock as he pushed himself past, it fell against him, hurting him in the ribs with the splintered bone of its upper arm. It was hatless, jawless, headed like a lizard of mud. He pushed

it away from him with an oath, and floundered
on. Help, help, the water was over his head. He
turned over in frantic choking darkness. He got
his head up, choking in screams of terror of being
drowned. A rifle was held out. He gripped the
butt, and hauled himself against the suck of the
shell-hole. I've l-l-lost me rifle, sir, he told the
officer, hoping that he would be sent back.
" Take the next wounded man's rifle." The
officer gave John Bullock a gulp of his water-
bottle which made him choke. Rum. " Stuff to
give 'em, sir." " For Christ's sake get a move on,

it's two o'clock already and we'll miss the blasted barrage." " Right you are, Sir." Lead on forever, left foot, right foot, blow wind, fire-spouting mud, wade on forever. He shouted to a couple of dead drivers by their smashed limber, lit up in the smoky red glare of an 8-inch bastard. Pull out the left foot, ankle sharp pain, flop, now the right leg, up she comes. Zzzzzzzuzz—CRASH : Down, and up again. " Hullo, chum, what's up, copped it ? " Nobby Clark was lying just off the track. " I'm done, Nosey. Go on, boy, good luck." John Bullock stood by him, trying to

shield him from the lash of the glinting rain. Another brutal whine dropped nearer. Splinters zipped over. " Where'r you hit, Nobby ? " " In back," gasped Nobby. " I'm done. Good luck, boy." Nobby rolled his head. His legs were twisted back under him. His head ceased to roll. Christ, poor old Nobby —. John Bullock rose up and trudged on towards the flares. At four o'clock in the morning the brigadier, with the colonel and adjutant, stood where the Cockroft track crossed the Poelcappelle road, outside a pillbox, brigade battle headquarters. " Stick it, men," said the colonel, " you're nearly there." The brigadier was thinking bitterly, Battle weather, the tanks won't be able to get up ; bloody, bloody rain, it always fell on Y/Z night, bitching the contract. The colonel shook hands with him, saluted, and went on with his battle adjutant. His battle headquarters were to be near the church ; so far, they existed only on the map. He longed to go over with his men, all the way with them ; in his fury against Army H.Q. he could have gone on and on until he had no battalion left to be b——d about by a lot of unimaginative brass-hats who had never come nearer the line than the last château, and then only after baths had been put into them. It was ——— murder, and the men knew it. The green-ish flares hissed up very high and near. Bullets cracked over the files of men as they wrenched their feet towards the hypothetical assembly tape. A steady low buzzing made John Bullock

look to the left. The dark shapes of tanks were
seen, one behind the other, moving towards the
ruins of the village. He forgot them in the dark,
timeless struggle of monstrous aching legs and
thumping heart. His blood was heavy and thick.
He was beyond thirst. Salvoes crashed on the
left, spouting smoke-red zizz-z-zz zinn-n-nn of
splinters. Then a yellow-forked narrow flame
rose to a great height along the road, showing
the faces of laden men in file lurching forward.
Dark figures around the tanks. Hot and sweating, clogged with half-a-hundredweight of mud,

John Bullock leaned his hands on his knees and watched the huge flames being blown by the wind. A tank on fire ! That's caused it ! Within a minute high explosive shells were falling in bunches of salvoes. Other forked flames in line, as though the poplars once lining the road were recreated in fire. The flaming poplars rose one behind the other into the light-roar. The rain was dimly realized by the slanting misty splashes on the lurid wastes before him. He watched them trying to turn round, great black toads. One tipped itself off the road and chugged

towards them. Petrol shells broke around it like waves on a reef. A proper bloody shell-trap. It stopped, bellied in a shell-hole. Its tracks raced round and round. On again, the groin-sinews grating as with broken glass, the heart filling the body from belly to throat. Sideway staggering aching heaviness. At last he could lie down and fade away in the ground. The greatest blessing, heedless of the swoop and crash of shells. Nothing mattered. He was all in. Fini. But very soon the cold grew into him from the ground, and he realized where he was, and after a minute's struggle, and lapses when he lay back and wept, he managed to get on his hands and knees, and, pressing against the unbalanced weights of his body, to press himself upright from his feet. He gliddered along to the next man, who was sitting in a shell-hole asleep. It was Trengrove. " Hey ? Hey ? " was all he replied. John Bullock hit him in the face. Trengrove numbed beyond teeth-chattering ; his jaw was set. John Bullock wept. " Get up, Trenny, we're —— lost," and he fell down beside him, and slept. He awoke to the sergeant shaking him. " Orficer ! " The officer gave him some rum. The officer spoke thickly and put his hand on John Bullock's shoulder. " Who cares a b——r, eh, ol' chap ? Have a drink. Stuff t'giv'm. Hey, don't drink it all, laddie." John Bullock realized the officer wasn't tight, only pretending. " Thank you, sir." " Took us eleven hours, Bullock. The barrage starts in half-an-hour." " I'm with you, sir, I managed to get a rifle, sir." "Good boy. Who's that, Trengrove? Here you are, laddie. Six per cent. overproof." The rum unsoddened John Bullock; he swung his arms almost cheerfully for another couple of minutes. It was strangely silent; the suck of his boots as he lifted his feet was loud. Where were the flares? Had Jerry pulled out and gone back. He slid down and slept again. The officer floundered back, without speaking. A hum in the darkness. Aeroplane. It swelled louder, flying very low; the engine made a snarling noise as it passed by only a few yards

up. More planes. The sergeant came splashing
along. " Don't fire at it," he cried in a loud
whisper, " don't fire." " Don't get wind up,"
murmured John Bullock into his box respirator.
Another passed behind them, and another. He
looked up into the frigid night. They passed over
higher up, and soon he saw flashes and a few
seconds later heard the remote reports of the
guns immediately before the swish and flash and
clanging crack of shrapnel. Wider flashes and
duller reports ; the prolonged wait, the slow,
coarse buzzing of big stuff. Machine-guns rattled
from the brewery at the farther end of the
village. Pss-pss-pss-pss, the bullets streaked
overhead. He sat on his heels within the upper
slopes of his shell-hole, waiting in a stupor of
unreality. " Hi, there, who says rum ? " The
company sergeant-major, D.C.M., and M.M. with
bar, five wound stripes, a small round-headed,
black-eyed man with the grin of the world-
hardened, was standing above, his tin hat
cocked over one ear. Other figures moved to him,
and took turns at the canteen. A runner stood
behind with the jar. The C.S.M. had drunk
nearly a pint of rum. " Fix bayonets, boys," he
said, grinning and showing his teeth, and speaking
with jerky, repressed fury in his voice. "Straight
in at the bastards. You know what to do to the
kamerards—kamerard them with three inches
in the throat, or if you miss, with the butt in the
———." He showed his terrible grin at a
salvo of 5.9's spouting sixty yards behind them,

and his lips covered and uncovered his teeth. He seemed to spring away through the mud, laughing, carrying his canteen of rum. John Bullock felt fine, the rum seemed to have taken all feeling out of him—cold, fear, fatigue. He felt only his eyes in the darkness above his body. His bayonet rasped out of its sheath, and locked grittily. Had he done that ? How ? He was aware of other bayonets glinting in the livid wavering light, among the luminous smoke drifting away from the rending glare of the enemy barrage. " How d'you feel, boy," shouted someone from under

the rim of a helmet. " All right ! " " So'm I."
" It ain't so bad as I'd thought it'd be." " No,
but I shan't be sorry when it starts." With
rifles slung, they beat their wooden hands on
their thighs. Half the sky leapt alight behind
them, there were shouts and cries, a cascade of
sound slipped solidly upon them, seeming to
John Bullock to swell and converge upon the
place where his now very trembling body was
large and alone. He saw a long pale shadow
before him an instant before it vagged and
vanished in the shock of the earth rushing up in
fire before him. He was aware of men going forward, himself with them, of the unreality of all
movement, of the barrage which was all-weight
and all-sound, so that he was carried forward
effortlessly over a land freed from the force of
gravity and matter. As in a nightmare of rising
green and white showers of light above the rending fire he shouted without sound in a silent
world, his senses fused into a glassy delirium
which lasted until he realized that of the figures
on either side of him some were slowly going
down on their knees, their chins on their box-
respirators, their rifles loosening from their
hands. He was hot and swearing, and his throat
was dried up. That sissing noise and far-away
racketting must be emma-gees. Now the fire
wall was going down under his nose and streaking sparks were over and he was lying on his
back watching a great torn umbrella of mud,
while his head was drawn down into his belly.

(The vacuum of a dud shell falling just behind him.) He retched for breath. His ears screamed in his head. He crawled to his knees and looked to see what had happened. Chaps going on forward. He was on his feet in the sissing criss-cross and stinking of smoking earth gaping— hullo, hullo, new shell-holes, this must be near the first objective. They had come three hundred yards already! Cushy! Nothing in going over the top! Then his heart instead of finishing its beat and pausing to beat again swelled out its beat into an ear-bursting agony and great lurid

light that leapt out of his broken-apart body
with a spinning shriek
and the earth was in his eyes and up his nostrils
and going away smaller and smaller
into blackness
and   tiny   far   away

   Rough and smooth. Rough was wide and large
and tilting with sickness. He struggled and
struggled to clutch smooth, and it slid away.
Rough came back and washed harshly over him.
He cried out between the receding of rough and
the coming of smooth white, then rough and

smooth receded. Thus the day and the night, the wind and the rain, as he lay, sometimes struggling for consciousness, beside the slight furrow made by the bursting of the 4.2 inch howitzer shell with instantaneous fuse. During the second day his eyes focussed on the rim of a tin-hat, and in desperate clutching to the sky through a swirl and sway of nausea he raised himself on an elbow and looked around. Ragged rough bore him down and smothered him. He glided away again, and opened his eyes into a starry sky, and felt the wildest fear, and cried out for his mother to save him. The stars were pale, the

sky flicked with livid flashes when he awakened
shivering and with his immense lolling hot head
thumping with shell bursts. He remembered the
C.S.M. and the low-flying planes, the barrage and
the attack. In wildest fear he screamed out
against DEATH. He could feel only his big aching head. Why was it only his head ? He heard
crying a long way from him and wondered if it
was his voice. He struggled to define himself, but
everything was so far away. The rough far-away
came nearer after blankness, when his head was
not so unwieldly large, and he saw his hand and

could just move it. Voices were tilting earth and sky. He heard one say, " This one's a stiff." He said, looking at a face bending over him, " Hullo, Daddy Washout." Daddy Washout stared at him. " He's alive, I saw one of his eyes move." And another voice said, " We won't 'arf cop it if they opens up on us. Look, that Jerry over there's waving 'is arm." John Bullock tried to tell them he was there, alive. Daddy Washout was peering anxiously at him. " It is John Bullock," said Daddy Washout. His face grew larger, John Bullock tried to speak. Daddy's legs were wrapped in sandbags. He wore a dirty white and creased band on his arm, marked with the red cross. " He may be living," said Daddy. " Take hold of his feet. Both together. Now ! " German and English stretcher-bearers were searching in the churned land, littered with rifles, equipment, cartridges, helmets, and lumps of grey and khaki in every position and still posture, some torn open showing bluish white flesh under broken pink and grey undervests, others bent back and sprawled all ways, gashed, ripped and crumpled. The four men, each clinging to a handle of the stretcher, now at arm's length, now on their shoulders, bore John Bullock's body to the battalion aid post. It was in a pill-box cracked and subsided in one corner, after being hit by a 12-inch shell. The cement interior was ankle-deep in slime, packed with wounded men, many dying, all stinking of corruption after lying out in the crater zone for three days and nights. A German machine-gun stood on an iron sled swivel in one corner, its cartridge belt jammed in its lock after the water in the cooling-jacket had boiled away. Chips of concrete as big as saucers and plates had flown from the inner walls under the weight of the shells' concussion. Light came through the machine-gun splayed slits at ground-level facing north and south and east, but not westwards towards the old British lines ; the doorway, with its fixed and buckled steel door, behind the pill-box, was open to the German shells. *Gott Strafe England* had been painted on the interior of the door by laughing German pioneers a year before; the corpses of the Germans who had surrendered when their machine-guns had jammed were trodden into the pug around the aid-post. " Cheero Boys," the padre, had worked round the post for three days and nights without sleep, constantly suppressing his fear, comforting whom he could. Never before had his mind felt so strong and clear; for he believed that Christ had come again to the world, arising in the comradeship of men crucified on the battlefields. He died of nervous exhaustion soon after the Armistice.

FIFTH PHASE

JOHN BULLOCK's leg, hanging by a stump of
septic flesh and sinew, having been severed by a
stretcher-bearer's jack-knife ; the stump having
been spattered with iodine and dressed ; anti-
tetanus serum having been injected into the
flaccid mottled thigh, a tourniquet of puttee and
shell-splinter turned ; he was covered with a
muddy blanket, and the stretcher was placed

beside others behind the pill-box. Several times
in the afternoon the cases were inspected to see
which were dead. Stretchers were needed. Late
in the afternoon some prisoners came down and
were told off as stretcher-bearers. The faces of
the Germans were toadstool-pale, some twitched
and glanced about them with wild eyes. Their
eye-balls were flaring with shell-bursts. Their
tunics hung slack. Their minds were hollow and
ravished. They staggered along the downward
duck-track laid parallel to and a hundred yards
away from the road. They passed upward-going
troops on the far side of the road. Shells were
bursting with airy puffs and black spoutings
near and far over the worm-dead watery wastes.
One of John Bullock's many-button'd-grey-
coated bearers fell jerking and champing in a
fit, and he was tipped off his stretcher. They
paused, wondering what to do ; shells groaned
down the sky, flinging their black fans of earth
and smoke ; they crouched, and propped the
inert man against a corpse, to keep his face out
of the mud until he should recover. The snor-
ing German was left behind ; the clot of figures
straggled on in file again. Hope was beginning to
flow into their ravished lives. Their spirits saw
freedom again, for every step was taking these
men out of the war. " Thank you, mates,"
whispered John Bullock, to the gasping Jerries
as they put down the stretcher to wait for the
ambulance. " Good luck, Tommee," said one, as
they stumbled away under escort.

Night shut down the waste land. Rough came back again. He sank under it, struggling. The stretcher slid into the iron grooves within the motor ambulance. His head was rolling; his hands were clawing the rough away from his

breathing. While the Ford ambulance was swaying and bumping along the St. Julien road in the darkness, passing the silent battalions going up for to-morrow's attack, an old man was reading in his Liberal daily newspaper an account of the latest fighting. To his wife in her chair on the other side of the fire, he read—

" *But the cry of ' No surrender ! ' was in the souls of these gallant men. They had no complaint against the fate that thrust them into the morass nor any whimper against their hard luck.*"

" Ah ! " said the mother, shaking her head.

" Listen ! " said Dad.

" *I have known nothing finer in this war than the quality of the talk I have heard among the men who fought all day after a night exposed in wild rain, and lay out all that night in water-pools under gun-fire, and came back again yesterday wounded, spent, bloody and muddy, cramped and stiff, cold to the marrow-bones, and tired after the agony of the long trail back across the barren fields. They did not despair because they had not gained all they had hoped to gain. ' We'll get it all right next time,' said man after man among them. They all stated the reasons for their bad luck. That faith, that confidence in their own fighting quality, was not dimmed because they had not gone far. The fire of it, the beauty of it, the simplicity of it shone in the eyes of these men, who were racked with aches and shot through with pain, all befouled by the mud, which was in the very pores of their skin, and seared by remembrances of tragic things.*"

The mother shook her head slowly.

" Listen to this, mother ! "

" *While I was talking to these men a figure came and sat on a bench among them, speech-*

*less, because no one understood his tongue. It
was a wounded German prisoner. Among all
these men of ours who spoke with a fine
hopefulness of what they would do next time,
he was hopeless. ' We are lost,' he said. ' My
division is ended. My friends are all killed. I
lay three days in a shell-hole—('ein granaten
loch')—and your men helped me out because I
was wounded. Your men are good. Your
artillery is good. It is very bad for us. We
are kaput.' "*

*" On the one side of the fire were the men
who think they are winning, whatever checks
they may have, and who always attack with
that faith in their hearts. On the other side
was the man who said, ' We are finished,' and
sat huddled up in despair. All of them had
suffered the same things."*

"English pluck, that's what it is," declared
the old man, in a voice of proud satisfaction, as
he stretched out his feet to the fire.

The wind against the window made a sudden
high shriek like mad laughter.

"Ah!" said the mother, wandering and
questing in the waste land of her mind. The wind
drove the rain hard on the window-pane, cur-
tained dark against air-raids ; the wind cried in
the cracks, and she heard the cries in the waste
land ; and she went to get the supper, and came
back smiling, for Dad was tired, staying late
every night because all the younger men had
gone from the works.

The wind drove the rain over the dark, crumbled hollows and rubble heaps of Ypres. Long-range high-explosive shrapnel cracked and drifted in woolly-bear smoke over the station where an ambulance train was waiting with anxious driver. Troops marched past, going up for another assault ; they marched silently ; troops of a division going into the battle for the fourth time. The lightly wounded on the train watched them silently, then turned away and drank hot, sweet, milky tea, in enamel mugs ; the rootlets of their minds growing in hope towards England.

The train stopped in the congested area of brown huts and grey marquees between Poperinghe and the low hills to the south. Here were three new stations, officially called Dosinghem, Bandaghem, and Mendinghem. Acres of wooden crosses stretching away from the sidings ; iodoform and gangrenous whiffs : fatigue burial parties working seven days a week : great cheer among the cushy Blighty ones. John Bullock had a glass of warm sugared milk, with egg and brandy in it. " Thank you, sister." He gave, between waves of blank pain, his number, name, and regiment. Gun-fire rolled along and flapped the canvas of the marquee. White doctors, yellow rubber gloves. Thermometer, mustn't bite it, aough ! he rolled his head with pain. Dimly realized the blankets peeling off and laid on whiteness, faces peering, electric light, snipping scissors swearing down his arm. He felt a prick

in his arm and his head buzzed, and he was clawing to get away from rough. He went right away
and swung back again and heard voices which
were near and yet far away again. Rough and
smooth. Hullo, Nobby boy, where've you been ?
Dodging the column ? Blimey, your haversack

and canteen's cut to rags, and your tin hat's like
a fire-bucket. Nobby, Nobby, what's up, mate ?
Nobby faded away, and the rough was up to his
knees moving slowly past him like an elephant's
skin, and the rain-prickles glittered in the watery
craters. He was hanging over the darkness

clawing at rough with a high shriek of mad laughter.

The surgeon, who had worked on an average of sixteen hours a day for the past two months, shook his head. " Put him in B Marquee," he

said. A pile of muddy blankets lay in the corner of B marquee, near the door. Each corpse was wrapped in one before being carried out to the cemetery. Every corpse had heard, or said at least once in his army life, ironically, " They even make you pay for the blanket they bury you in ! " Cries and screams, groans and wild laughter : the marquee flapped with wind and rippled with gun-fire. Trains rolled past, miles of grey lorries, the never ceasing rattle of waggon wheels, ambulances, masked lights. In the morning he was still alive when the burial fatigue, B2 soldiers of a labour company, damp and fed-up from twelve in a tent, looked in. And so he was evacuated, put on the next train to the base, with a ticket tied to the second button of his tunic : number, name, regiment, and the letters " G.S.W. (Gun shot wound). Left arm, abdomen, buttocks, etc." Groans, cries, and counter-cries.

Water, water, for Christ's sake. Why can't a
bloke get a bit of sleep. Orderly, bring a bottle,
please. Water, water. In, out, on guard. Give
'em hell, boys. Help, help, for God's sake don't
leave me. Aoh! For Gawd's sake put a sock in
it! Where're we going, orderly? Rouen, my
God, I've been out of bed for three days and
nights. Don't take it to heart, laddie, it's worse
for the boys in the line. Help, help, I can't get
out, don't leave me, sir. The train glided on
through the howling darkness, and in the morning they were taken to No. 4 General Hospital,

which the Germans had used in 1870 for their wounded. The terrible silence of the white wards, the swish of felt slippers, the terrible white walls and crying, the strange white sheets and beds in a row. Terrible silence at night, beyond the cries and groans in the ward, the throb and ache, ache, ache, of his right foot. Bare blank ceiling, sparks passing across, up and down, and across, up and down, long, long, grey-darkness of night. Whispers and lights round the next bed, then the screams ; and the stretcher. Orderly, are we going home ? Rough and smooth, the fretted rising of rough and the glaring blast all over the world. Nobby, Nobby, what's up with your haversack and tunic, torn to shreds, Nobby. The blurred light and whisper, the prick in the arm, the gliding away on lovely smooth. Then the burning throb of his leg and the gurgling suck of the red rubber tube within the wooden cage around his leg. Afternoon, brandy, egg and milk, jolly fine stuff, feeling better. Ticket marked BUNK on his nightshirt. No more football or games, but he would get O.K. the doctor said. Well, he wasn't sorry to be out of it. Trees on the banks, going Havre, they said. Soup for dinner. Aough ! no good, blast the pain, like one great toothache in his leg *that wasn't there*. The sea journey in darkness became dim-realized in patches, and went on and on. Blighty at last, chaps looking out of the round glass windows, lucky chaps, got cushy Blighties. They would return ! Hollow fear stirred in him, although he

wouldn't go back. Long, everlasting train journey, rough again and bursting head. Mum and
Dad were looking at him, Dad asking, smiling,
how he was. All right, Dad. Mum, smiling and
crying. " No, no, I mustn't cry," she muttered,
and tried only to smile. Black grapes ; why waste
money on black grapes, he asked, petulantly.
Green are cheaper, and just as nice. " Yes, dear,"
whispered Mum. Poor old Mum and Dad, they
didn't know anything. " Well, did you shoot any
Huns ? " asked Dad, beaming and proud and
rather timidly. " I didn't see one," he cried.

" Didn't see one, I bet," said Dad, proud and knowing. I tell you I DIDN'T, he shrieked suddenly, and the nurse came and said he must sleep now, and Mum stroked his hair, and John Bullock's face was puckered and shaking with sobs. His father, standing by the bed, hat in hand, looked sad and bewildered.

Months and months of pain and contentment : regular grub and fags, military band outside once a week, and sometimes a theatre, riding in a toff's car. The stump healed clean. He grew fat and happy, and lost all interest in the war.

Never wanted to hear of it again. It hadn't been such a bad time, taken all round : he wouldn't have missed it, really. They said you could do a lot on an artificial leg.

In his suit of hospital blue, with trouser turned up showing six inches of white lining, and red tie, John Bullock used to swing himself along on his single leg between crutches, to sit in the public park, sometimes with some of the boys, sometimes by himself. He was contented, watching the couples on the grass, and talking to children. He was out in the street on 11th Novem-

ber, waiting for the maroons to go off at eleven
o'clock, when an old toff stopped him and asked
him how he had lost his leg. John Bullock told
him. A five-nine, as we were going over. The toff
soon lost interest, and when the flags were
waving, he said : " Well, I suppose it's a good
thing it's over, but in my opinion the Govern-
ment is weak. We ought to have driven the Huns
back into Berlin, and given their country
a taste of what they gave France."

" Ah ! " said John Bullock, shifting on his leg.

" However," said the old gentleman, giving
him a cigar, as he prepared to move on, to see

the fun. Whistles were blowing, people shouting and singing, motor horns honking, and a deuce of a fine old row everywhere. " We always did do things in England by halves." At this moment a very little boy ran up, waving a flag : and seeing his daddy talking to someone, he stopped. " Look, daddy, look ! " cried the little boy. " The poor man hasn't got only one boot on ! "

" Ssh ! You mustn't notice such things ! " said the toff. "This good man is a hero. Yes," he went on, "we'll see that England doesn't forget you fellows."

" We are England," said John Bullock, with a slow smile. The old gentleman could not look him in the eyes ; and the little boy ceased to wave his flag, and stared sorrowfully at the poor man.

HERE ENDS
THE PATRIOT'S PROGRESS
WHICH WAS CUT IN LINO BY
WILLIAM KERMODE AT KEW
GARDENS IN SURREY IN MCMXXIX
WRITTEN BY HENRY WILLIAMSON
IN THE VILLAGE OF HAM IN
DEVON IN THE SAME YEAR
PRINTED BY THE EUSTON PRESS
AT FOUR EUSTON BUILDINGS
IN NORTH - WEST LONDON AND
PUBLISHED BY GEOFFREY BLES AT
TWENTY-TWO SUFFOLK STREET
PALL MALL LONDON MCMXXX